Christian Strategy in the Television Age

Other books by Colin Morris:

The Hour after Midnight
Out of Africa's Crucible
Include Me Out
Unyoung, uncoloured, unpoor
Mankind, My Church
The Hammer of the Lord
Epistles to the Apostle
The Word and the Words
Get Through till Nightfall

GOD-IN-A-BOX

*Christian Strategy in the
Television Age*

Colin Morris

HODDER AND STOUGHTON
LONDON   SYDNEY   AUCKLAND   TORONTO

254.3

British Library Cataloguing in Publication Date

Morris, Colin, *1929–*
  God in a box.——(Hodder Christian paperbacks)
  1. Television in religion 2. Television
in education 3. Christian education
  I. Title
  207'.153   BV656.3

ISBN 0 340 33865 2

2002990∠

*Hodder and Stoughton Editorial Office: 47 Bedford Square,
London WC1B 3DP*

Preface

Some books are written to be superseded. This is one. I greatly hope some reader will be impelled or provoked to do the job better. There is endless scope – some of the area covered is largely unexplored territory. Neither the Churches nor the academic theological community has yet made any systematic attempt to colonise it.

This is a voyage of discovery made by someone who, late in his career, took ship for a strange new world. Because I came to the BBC after twenty-five years mostly spent as a missionary in Africa, things that were old hat to others in Britain were as newly minted treasure to me. For instance, I first encountered the ideas of Marshall McLuhan a full decade after just about everyone else had discarded them.

There is the odd advantage to limping along behind the column. One is free to make discoveries unburdened by the conventional wisdom; to see through fresh eyes things which for others have become an unremarked part of the landscape.

Because all voyages of discovery are intensely personal, some of the things one sees turn out to be mirages; other things one doesn't see at all. This the reader must take into account.

I have only briefly mentioned radio in this book. This is not because I think of it is an unimportant force in the electronic revolution. Quite the contrary. For the purpose of exploring ideas and stimulating the imagination without dragooning it, radio is unequalled. Quite simply, I haven't dealt with radio because I don't know enough about it. There are plenty of people around who do; I hope they will repair my omission.

I have acknowledgments to make. Pauline Webb did not allow our long and close friendship to cloud her editorial judgment. She read three drafts with equal care, dealt mercilessly with woolly thinking or slipshod expression and the book is clearer, sharper and briefer as a consequence. Then there is Dr W.F. Dillistone, the doyen of British theologians currently thinking and writing about communication. He is a great encourager of those less equipped than himself to wrestle with major theological themes. I benefited greatly both in conversation and correspondence with him.

The Barr brothers, Andrew and Jeremy engaged me in penetrating debate and each brought much television expertise to bear on my ideas. Father Robert White and James McConnell of the Centre for the Study of Communication and Culture used their encyclopaedic knowledge of the literature of the field to direct me to books and papers which might be of value. The British Churches have not yet realised what a priceless resource they possess in the Centre for the Study of Communication and Culture and in its Director, Bob White.

I owe much to my colleagues in the BBC's Television Service from whose highly knowledgeable and articulate discussions about television programmes and policies in the Programme Review Board I have learned most of what I know about the subject.

The BBC gave me the opportunity to make this voyage of discovery and imposed on me no preconditions other than a concern for excellence and humility before the truth. It goes without saying that any opinions in this book are my own and the BBC bears no responsibility for them.

Finally, with endless patience and efficiency, Jean Palk typed every draft. She knows how much I owe her.

Colin Morris
BBC Television Centre
London W12

Contents

This book is for

Harry Morton –

a Giant, felled

Introduction

This book is about a revolutionary take-over of society accomplished without a shot being fired. The local agent of the revolution sits demurely in your sitting-room, staring at you, glassy-eyed – your television set. That may seem a lot to claim for a gadget generally thought of only as a medium of entertainment or even as a sophisticated toy.

So don't take my word for it. The historian, David Boorstin, who is Librarian of the US Congress and therefore presumably not given to flights of wild rhetoric, has said, 'The crisis of our time, the next great crisis of human consciousness, has come with television.' Another expert, Larry Grossman, when President of the Public Broadcasting System of the United States, turned to science fiction and chose a term from the movie *Star Wars* by which to describe television. It is, he claimed, The Force. He continued:

> Television is the frame in which we view the dimensions of our society. It reflects the quality of our culture and the character of our priorities. It is a determining influence on our politics, our economics, our ethics, our aesthetics, as well as our psychological and social perceptions.[1]

Some perceptive people saw the first stirrings of this electronic revolution a long time ago. In 1938, when television was in its infancy, E. B. White wrote in *The New Yorker*:

> I believe television is going to be the test of the modern world, and that in this new opportunity to see beyond the range of our vision we shall discover either a new and unbearable disturbance

of the general peace or a saving radiance in the sky. We shall stand or fall by television – of that I am sure.

In 1948, Grace Wyndham Goldie who left the Civil Service to become the first Head of BBC Television Talks and Current Affairs, took a quick look at her new environment and commented succinctly, 'Television is a bomb about to burst!' And in the 'sixties, Marshall McLuhan, the first scholar to spell out just what is so revolutionary about television wrote:

> As long as our technologies were as slow as the wheel or the alphabet or money, the fact that they were separate closed systems was socially and psychically supportable. This is not true now when sight and sound and movement are simultaneous and global in extent. We now face a crisis quite new in human history.

'Nonsense!' cry the enemies of television, usually highly civilised people who find unbelievable such high-falutin talk about the importance of the square-eyed monster. TV, they insist, offers only a pathetic world of escapism and fantasy, a domestic Disneyland where mesmerised viewers gawp uncomprehendingly at much of what they see like opium smokers staring at the wall.

They underestimate their enemy's power. Television is not in the business of offering an escapist alternative to the real world. Where television is, there *is* the real world. The medium has the ability to impose its view of reality on everyone who comes within range of its signals, as I shall try to show.

Granted, there are significant numbers of people in our society who go for weeks without watching a television programme. My point is that they do not go for a day without their lives being shaped by the culture television is creating. Television's impact cannot be measured in crude statistical terms by the number of people who own television sets.

Television will not go away if we keep our eyes shut long enough. It is not a cock-eyed invention like the coal-fired moon rocket or the left-handed spanner – destined to end up in a museum of industrial archeology. Television is doing for human perception what the wheel did for feet. And like the invention of the wheel, its appearance marks a decisive turning-point in human history.

Television's influence is all-pervasive. It is not simply a device like a vacuum cleaner which serves us; it is an environment that wraps us round like a blanket.

For centuries human beings have lived in an atmosphere saturated by words – spoken, written, carved in wood and stone, fly-posted, printed, sung, broadcast and prayed. We and our ancestors have launched uncountable words into the air just as a plant excretes carbon dioxide or a factory chimney puffs out smoke.

We have both enriched and polluted this artificial atmosphere. At worst, we have almost choked in a verbal fog; at best we have inhaled the pure air of human expression at its most precise. Because this environment cannot be detected by our senses many of us have never realised it is there, just as a fish is probably not conscious of the water through which it swims.

Now this verbal environment is in the process of being transformed. For the first time in five hundred years, the word is no longer the dominant force in shaping our culture. The atmosphere flashes with the rich imagery of television. This does not mean that words have stopped being important, but they do not predominate. The image, chiefly projected through the television screen, is now the most powerful way of transmitting our culture.

Of course, we have never been able to pluck words from the verbal environment and use them raw, as it were, in communication. They needed to be decoded first. Cultural codes such as the rules of grammar and syntax have been necessary to convert the contents of our environment into messages.

But here is the rub. Whereas we have had five centuries to master the cultural codes which apply to words, we are all at sea in the environment which television is transforming. To distil communication from tele-culture's ceaseless swirl of image and word still requires a code. And we have not yet discovered what it is. So we are adrift in mental space with an out-of-date code book.

And to make matters worse, because television has such power of feedback, it is like some electronic monster busily devouring the factory which produced it. It is swallowing the very culture from which we derive the codes that might enable us to understand its signals.

What will this cultural transformation do to the people caught up in it? Theologians are fond of trying to tie a neat label to contemporary man which purports to catch in a phrase his key characteristic. For instance a US theologian, Harvey Cox, notes the appearance in our time of 'post-literate man'. The Age of Writing is over, he says. The visual electronic image has replaced the written word as the crucial unit of communication.

As the post-literate person evolves, his or her world-view will differ radically from that of the Age of Writing, just as that Age's perceptions were different from those of pre-literate verbal cultures. Any revolutionary change in the technology of communication demands more than new skills and aptitudes; it requires a new way of perceiving reality.

The practical effect of this will be felt particularly by those engaged in the communications business who have been used to thinking in words and constructing verbal systems of ideas – theologians and politicians, for instance. To reach the post-literate person they will have to wrestle primarily with images – reframing rather than rephrasing their messages.

Because you do not need to be able to read and write to receive and understand television signals, it is not necessary to be educated in order to be informed. Teachers of young children know this better than most. Children do not bring to school innocent, empty heads to be filled with knowledge during their lessons. They arrive on their very first day at school with their heads already bursting with information gleaned from watching television. It is, of course, unclassi-fied knowledge, neither sorted out nor critically appraised;

simply absorbed indiscriminately from moment to moment.

Some of this pre- and extra-school knowledge is quickly forgotten, a lot more has been misunderstood and therefore does not count as knowledge at all. But the overall effect is to abolish a virtual monopoly educationalists have enjoyed for centuries. The teacher has traditionally not only decided the range of knowledge children could encompass at different ages but also the speed at which they were allowed to explore it. No longer.

An even more remarkable example of a telescoping of eras of communication was demonstrated when television arrived in the Third World. Whole cultures leap-frogged from pre-literate to post-literate stages of development without pausing to absorb the intermediate stage of book-learning.

I was a missionary on the Zambian Copperbelt in the 1960s when television arrived. An astonishing cultural revolution occurred. Young Africans who, a few months before the television station was set up, were unable to read and got their information from village gossip, were soon aping the dress and mannerisms of US television characters with total naturalness. Tribesmen for whom the inhabitants of the next village were strangers began to discuss world affairs with a degree of sophistication that was startling.

My point is not that television in Zambia or anywhere else has made it unnecessary for people to learn to read and write. The post-literate person is not necessarily or usually illiterate. But reading and writing no longer provide his or her initial orientation to reality.

Up to now, television has usually been regarded as an information source for leisure-time purposes. But the box of tricks in the corner of the sitting-room will become the focus of new patterns of work and social relationships.

Our society is on the brink of a cultural explosion which will be centred on the television screen but linked to a whole supermarket of gadgetry – the telephone, word processor, computer, video-recorder and laser beam. They will provide us with an electronic nervous system through which will pulse a virtually infinite quantity of information.

So many filaments of our lives will thread in and out of the television receivers dotted around our homes that it is only a matter of time before certain types of work revert, for the first time in over a century, to being cottage industries. Some classes of worker such as professionals – doctors, dentists, music teachers, chiropodists and so on – have traditionally operated from home. They are destined to be joined by people in the general line of administration and office operations. These will be the house-bound workers of the future.

The rough rule of thumb is that if it is possible to computerise a process then the work can be done just as easily at home as in the office. The computer terminal is no further from the one than the other as the crow or, at least, electrical impulse flies. Thus there will be eliminated the hassle of commuting costs, wear and tear on nerves and wasted travelling time.

Office tasks which are strictly routine, such as recording data, typing, general bookkeeping, preparing invoices and the like, are already candidates for the revolution in work location. Those tasks which demand face-to-face transactions and qualitative judgment await more sophisticated versions of the present two-way video systems. They are on the way.

One astonishing statistic is worth pondering. In the last thirty years, the proportion of the Gross National Product of the United States spent on the provision and movement of information in all its forms has risen from 15 to 40 per cent. Almost half the astronomic sum America generates by way of wealth each year is dedicated to an intangible product – not a thing but a process.

A rapidly growing proportion of the work-force of the Western world is engaged in packaging information rather than commodities. No longer do these workers handle *things* – making, storing, selling, repairing and disposing of them. These are processes which demand great space, heavy capital investment, high transportation costs and a big work-force. Instead, these workers deal with an intangible resource, information, which can be directed from place to place by remote control.

This vision of tomorrow's worker *communicating* rather than *commuting* to work excites the social planner unable to contain the transportation explosion in big cities and towns – with its inevitable fall-out of clogged roads, over-stretched public services, inadequate parking spaces and soaring fuel costs. It also appeals to the ecologist who notes that the motor car is the largest consumer of energy and the biggest single cause of air pollution in our society.

It would be silly to underestimate the radical shift in social attitudes and deeply ingrained customs required to create this electronic cottage industry centred on the television receiver. Even the physical and psychological environment of the home will have to be changed if domestic congestion indoors is not to replace traffic congestion outside.

Alvin Toffler in his latest work of social prophecy, *The Third Wave*, puts it this way:

> We cannot today know if, in fact, the electronic cottage will become the norm of the future. Never-the-less, it is worth recognising that if as few as 10 to 20 per cent of the work force as presently defined were to make this historic transfer over the next 20 or 30 years, our entire economy, our cities, our ecology, our family structure, our values, and even our politics, would be altered beyond recognition.[2]

This electronic spider's web can be constructed piecemeal *now* from combinations of gadgetry we already possess. There is no new revolutionary concept such as the wheel or nuclear energy still waiting to be invented. The computer can be married to the typewriter and television receiver to give birth to the domestic word processor. Or the television receiver plus the computer and telephone or cable line offers viewdata – a system for calling up and screening stored information in the form of maps, symbols, diagrams and pictures.

In sum, if television can revolutionise our working patterns and locations, it is hard to think of an area of human life which the beam of the cathode ray tube will not reach into and change. Christians have a particular responsibility to stare unflinchingly back at the probing electronic eye. They must try to make sense of what is happening as part of their prophetic duty to society as a whole. And they will inevitably speculate on their own future as a body of believers.

The hard religious questions press in. How can the Gospel be preached to a post-literate society in which the image is the principal currency of communication? How will Protestants especially, who proudly claim the title of People of the Book, fare when they encounter head-on the People of the Screen? What will be the fate of the Church as a community if the ultimate privatisation of society takes place around the domestic god with the square eye in its forehead? Can any belief in the transcendent survive the new electronic Babel?

And so on and on. Such questions might decently preoccupy successions of Vatican Councils or a conclave of theologians meeting in perpetual session for several generations. My intention is more modest. I want to look into the engine-room of the television leviathan and sketch out its essential dimensions so that we may know what manner of thing we are dealing with.

My chief authority for having any opinions about the matter is derived from the fact that I am, in the jargon of modern espionage, a mole. One of Them. I help to tend the square-eyed monster which is devouring our present culture. So by all means treat my conclusions with the utmost caution. But don't, I beg of you, underestimate the power of that innocuous little piece of furniture in the corner of your sitting-room. It truly is a force.

But not *the* force. Television is one of the most powerful of the principalities and powers – those secular institutions which are not under the Church's thumb but still within the range of God's sovereignty. And it is by wrestling with principalities and powers that Christians achieve true spiritual maturity.

This book falls into three parts. First, there is a guided tour through the curious world of television and the culture it is busy creating. Then I consider the special problems and challenges presented by religious television. Finally, I offer some thoughts about Christian mission in the Television Age.

PART ONE

_____

THE WORLD OF TELEVISION

ONE

The Names They Call Television

I begin this conducted tour of the world of television with a look at the public's perception of the medium. The sheer range of things television is likened to, the metaphors employed to describe it, indicate how deeply our culture and language have been penetrated by the machine and its ethos.

The Electronic Hearth
From the earliest times, the fire's warm glow has served as a rallying-point for the family. They gathered round the hearth to exchange news and gossip, to tell stories and make plans. Various members might have their own private domains – kitchen, potting-shed or nursery – but everyone collected beside a fire whose warmth and light were symbolic of family life at its best.

In many modern homes, the open hearth has been replaced by an impersonal and peripherally sited central-heating radiator. The family room has lost its traditional focal point. A quite special light has been dimmed in the interests of efficient heating.

Now the family room has gained a new centre, an electronic hearth that glows and flashes and attracts communal attention for much of the time – the television receiver. It is not just as a design feature that the set usually dominates the room. Its prominence symbolises a startling truth. Significant numbers of people now spend more hours every week watching television than doing any other thing, including working and sleeping.

The electronic hearth has created a strangely paradoxical

form of dispersed community. Throughout society television screens glow in almost every home, inducing identical interests in physically separated families. The old distinction between private and public activity has become blurred.

In the old days, if you wished to immerse yourself in community life, you went to church, the cinema, a concert, the theatre, a sports ground or pub. This was called social activity. What went on in your home was private, individual and random in timing and content. You chose your own life-agenda which probably coincided with that of other families only at the common junctions such as meal-times and hours of sleep.

On July 29th, 1981, 1,100 million people throughout the entire world followed an identical timetable and shared the same experience as they watched the Royal Wedding on television. But in their own homes. Was this public or private activity? The old definitions are no longer apt.

The word 'religion' is sometimes used in a debased sense to mean anything which is falsely elevated beyond its true worth. If the word is strictly applied, as its Latin root suggests, to that which binds human beings together most fundamentally, then television as the electronic hearth qualifies as some sort of religion.

For the first time since Roman households had domestic gods called the penates, the electronic hearth is the source of a people's religion which has no necessary connection with ecclesiastical institutions.

People's religion has always embraced stories told around the fire about heroes and ghosts, devils and saints, crude passions and purest love. And by means of these stories, adherents have had their perceptions informed, their conduct guided and their loyalties engaged.

One sociological definition of religion runs: that cluster of memories and myths, hopes and images, rites and customs which pulls together the life of a person or group into a significant whole. Television does this only in a highly stylised and derivative manner, but it is still the nearest that millions of people beyond the ambit of traditional religions get to an integrating experience.

In traditional people's religion, the nub of the matter had to do with living, loving, dying, giving birth, planting, hunting, reaping, playing and praying – the very themes reflected in the glow of the television screen for hour after hour. The electronic hearth may not be much of a sacred place, but it's the only one many people possess.

The Modern Traveller's Breviary

Father Alphonse Perrier, a Roman Catholic missionary priest, wrote to his brother from the depths of the Congo in 1891. After confessing his loneliness in the desolate, sultry valley where he had started building a mission station, he goes on:

> I am all alone with God and my breviary. That is not as grim as it sounds. Where that book is, I feel surrounded by a cloud of witnesses. What used to be something of an irksome routine (saying the Daily Office) has become a wonderful evocation of the life of Heaven and of a much loved world I fear I shall not see again with the eyes of the flesh... St-Sulpice in the height of a Parisian summer, the great West window aflame; the earnest voices of well-scrubbed schoolboys; the grave professors and earnest students at the Seminary...
>
> All these things come back to me as I recite the familiar and now so precious words. This magic beyond the wit of a native sorcerer – a whole vanished world leaps out of the covers of a tattered well-thumbed book...

That little book of prayers carried by Catholics on their journeyings, the breviary, contains more than the Daily Office, it radiates nostalgia. The language rings familiarly on the ear, the sentiments soothe the spirit and the mind is at home in that thought-world. The breviary symbolises the Old Church and the Old Faith. It holds the echo of the voices of parents, mentors and friends.

The television set is the breviary of modern man. In a strange city, the wayfarer settles into his room, remarking glumly the notices in a foreign language and the strange decor. Then he switches on the television set and is bathed in images and sounds he recognises and is at home with.

Television has become one of the few stable factors in a highly mobile global culture. As people move across the world they feel less strange wherever they set down because no matter how many thousand miles they have travelled they are only an arm's length away from an experience they are sharing with family and neighbours at home.

I have watched episodes of that quintessentially English drama, 'The Forsyte Saga', in the capitals of three African cities. In Saigon, South Vietnam, I sat in the lounge of a deserted hotel during the Viet Cong offensive of 1969 and watched on television the vintage comedy, 'Sergeant Bilko'. On the streets outside the hotel real US soldiers were dodging real bullets. But the world of Sergeant Bilko seemed much the more authentic of the two because it was a series I had watched regularly in Zambia.

Of course, the language of popular British series shown on foreign television channels will not always be familiar to the British traveller. Countries with sophisticated television systems which import major British and American programmes can afford to 'dub' the original actors' or commentators' voices into the local language.

Hence, on Tokyo television, Hilda Ogden and her neighbours in 'Coronation Street' jabber away happily in Japanese. The words they utter may be mystifying to the English-speaking visitor, but the gestures, background and atmosphere are unmistakable and speak of home.

It takes more than an unfamiliar sound-track to destroy completely the ethos of a well-known and loved television series. Those who disbelieve this should turn down the sound control of their television sets and watch the mute programmes. The result may not be very satisfactory, but marooned in a small town in Outer Mongolia, many bored exiles would prefer 'Crossroads' with a Ural-Altaic sound-track to a close-up view of the hotel bedroom wallpaper.

The strong-minded traveller might insist he welcomed the absence of English-language television in Outer Mongolia so that he could catch up on his serious reading. The rest would acknowledge that television is more than words and images. It is a cosmos, a created order, a pattern of sequences – news, drama, comedy, commercials and so on – whose totality spells familiarity even if individual bits are incomprehensible.

The Box

We tend to call the television receiver the Box when we are thinking of it as a piece of furniture to be hidden behind fretted doors or flaunted on a stand according to taste. We are so accustomed to shifting the box around the room to fit in with the décor that we may not realise how crucially important to the history of communication it was the first time someone moved a television set away from the wall.

Classical scholars may note the similarities between this momentous act and the emergence of the *kouros*.[3] *Kouros* was the name given to a type of Greek sculpture of the nude male first attributed to Polymedes of Argos in the sixth century BC. The *kouroi* were so original and important because they were free-standing. A new medium had been born; sculpture had finally parted company from its parent form, architecture – represented by the wall.

Before the *kouros*, sculpted figures were placed flat against a wall or created as a frieze round a wall. Sometimes they made up the entire building, walls and all. As an art, sculpture was still dependent upon and subordinate to another art, architecture.

The free-standing statue was a new form of visual communication achieved by incorporating the space round an object into the message of the object itself. This in turn led to two other innovations. Free-standing statues which were not an integral part of a building could be moved. Once they became portable, private ownership of them was made easier.

You might not be able to afford a whole temple, one frieze of which incorporated the figure you were interested in, nor could you easily demolish the whole building and move it elsewhere. But separate the figure from its setting and possession of it was a real possibility. You needn't visit the temple in order to appreciate the message of the sculpture;

you could place it in your own home and study it privately.

Portability and privacy are two crucial elements in the
development of communication. Take the spread of the
telephone. The poor have to queue for a public phone-box
while the affluent not only have a telephone in each room of
their homes but also one in their motor car for good measure.
The phone in the car is a perfect symbol of both portability
and privacy.

Then there is the current vogue for young people to walk
around playing a transistor radio or tape recorder attached to
headphones. Every day on the street we see this evidence of
perfect portability combined with utter privacy – the latest
development of communication techniques.

The earliest television-set owners tended to look upon
television as a novel variant of their home cinemas – those
specially equipped rooms with a projector behind one wall
and a screen on the wall opposite. Hence, the television set
was fixed against the room wall or sometimes built into it as
a substitute for the cinematograph screen. But once the
receiver was moved away from the wall several consequences
followed.

A television receiver – the box – was no longer a
continuation of the structure of the room (as a screen on the
wall was) but a discrete object in its own right. As a separate
object, it became more closely identified with the persona of
the owner and less with his enclosed space – just as a hot-
water bottle is more firmly linked to its owner than a central-
heating radiator which seems to belong to the bedroom like
the other fixtures and fittings.

The television set which is a personal object and not one
of the fittings of the room becomes both portable and
private. The box can easily be moved upstairs by a teenager
who wants to watch 'Top of the Pops' without the
accompaniment of adult comments of derision. And granny
in the old people's home is able to watch 'Songs of Praise'
all by herself on a portable set in her bedroom. Unless she
wishes to, she does not have to share a communal set in the
residents' television room.

A whole theory about the development of communication

can be based upon the free-standing position of a television set in your living-room.

The Memory Machine

A fifteen-year-old boy was giving a radio interview after being found alive in a cellar following a hurricane on the West Coast of America. 'When the big wind came,' he said, 'we knew just what to do because we had seen it so often on television.' This illustrates one of the pervasive though little noticed effects of television – its ability to create an artificial memory for the viewer. He can recall events and experiences which never happened to him in the real world because television furnishes him with an electronic past.

Here is another example. 'Though I had never travelled north of the Trent before, I recognised immediately the line of dull, dreary back-to-back dwellings, the occupants of which wear hair-nets or cloth caps, and spend their entire lives drinking stout in the pub or eating fish and chips at home.' That is how a reporter describes his first visit to Salford in Lancashire. He goes on to thank 'Coronation Street' for giving him this artificial familiarity with northern culture.

We give the name *déjà vu* to this feeling of having been in some place or passed through some experience before without knowing how or when it could have happened. It was once an aptitude confined to the more psychically sensitive personality; we are all now capable of experiencing it because of television.

Unlike earlier means of communication, television does not transport bits of information. It transports the viewer. It takes his spirit on a trip, and one dimension through which he journeys is the past, an artificially created but much richer experience than he could otherwise have known.

Quite frequently we do not consciously attribute this sense of *déjà vu* to television because we are unable to recall much of what we see on the screen. A television picture is a mass of unclassified information. This information is fired at us much too swiftly for us to register all its component parts. But the mind takes the information on board and may regurgitate it even though we think we have forgotten it.

A corollary of *déjà vu* is the capacity of television to re-educate a society's corporate memory. That is another way of saying television rewrites history. Personalities and events of the past are revisualised by television and burned into our memories, obliterating all previous impressions.

Dozens of biographies have been written about T. E. Lawrence, but Peter O'Toole's interpretation of the role in the film *Lawrence of Arabia* has become the accepted wisdom about this strange man. Only scholars will now care that the truth is more complex, diffuse and ambiguous than that offered in David Lean's beautifully simple and neatly plotted film. Sir Thomas More has now become *The Man for All Seasons* and Zeffirelli's *Jesus of Nazareth* is the new authorised biography in the minds of millions, let the protests of New Testament scholars be never so strident.

Television not only rewrites history, it usurps the literary imagination. Margaret Mitchell's *Gone with the Wind* was a novel long before it was filmed, but who can read it now without visualising a Scarlett O'Hara who looks like Vivien Leigh or a Rhett Butler created in Clark Gable's image? Soames Forsyte of the *Forsyte Saga* has many personality quirks in the book which are not carried over into Eric Porter's portrayal in the televised dramatisation. They are lost for ever. It is now the television producer's Soames, and not that of John Galsworthy, who is fixed in the memories of millions.

There was a past era when television did not exist. There is no past era which television is not busy recreating.

The Medium as Minstrel
One of the most illuminating images of television is that of the minstrel or electronic bard.[4] The bards were the minstrels of the ancient Celtic peoples, the Gauls, British, Welsh, Irish and Scots. These tribal dignitaries celebrated the deeds of gods and heroes, stirred up the people for battle and recorded tribal history in verse.

The bards were the incarnate memory-banks of the Celts. They survived in Ireland and Wales, two nations of compulsive gossips, story-tellers and natural talkers, long after they had disappeared elsewhere. The traditional bard, though he appeared before the people in the guise of a popular entertainer, had a more complex role. He was the arbiter of language, coining metaphors and phrases which reinforced the tribe's identity and marked it off from its neighbours.

Bards were not intended to be prophets, confronting the people with unpalatable truths they would rather dodge. Nor were they usually the originators of the compositions which emerged from the creative depths of the tribal soul. They were mediators of a body of truth and lore which belonged to the people but might be lying around gathering dust in some crevice of the collective memory.

The bard's originality lay in his skill as a communicator rather than in any virtuosity as a composer. He addressed the people from the centre of the culture, not from its edges.

Television's role as a creator of cultural consensus accords well with that summary description of the bardic office. Television gathers the people together and reinforces the way they perceive themselves. The electronic bard reflects society; it does not normally attempt to confront it.

There is a popular fictional plot which has some power-hungry zealot exploiting television to transform the decent, moderate masses into howling extremists. That is pure fantasy. The chances of television challenging deeply-held convictions or driving the mass of viewers from the political centre to the fringes of society, left or right, are remote.

The reason for television's in-built moderation is technical rather than ideological. It has to do with the nature of mass communication. Unlike preaching, teaching or public oratory, in broadcasting, neither party – the communicators nor the communicated with – knows who the other party is. Therefore, the only way the professionals can ensure that they are firmly in touch with the vast undifferentiated mass of viewers or listeners is to strike for the central meaning systems of the culture.

To base a broadcasting policy, as opposed to the odd programme, on the transmission of what is novel, original

or exotic, is to risk a massive act of non-communication. So
viewers will usually be protected from the unfamiliar, the
violently partisan and the very eccentric. Their self-image
will be strengthened, not undermined, by the electronic
bard.

Some conservatives view the media with great suspicion
as hotbeds of left-wing radicals. They are hard to convince
that television fulfils a minstrel role encouraging social
cohesion. Yet observation suggests that television's controlling philosophy is a vague and misty liberalism.

On television, good more or less triumphs over evil,
everything just about works out right in the end; complexities are, on balance, simplified and opposing opinions
get fairly stated with none of them allowed to dominate.
People tend to do the decent thing, and in the spectrum of
mood which ranges from optimism to despair, the needle
settles a little shakily in the sunny sector.

No awful human calamity such as famine, earthquake or
war is allowed to burn its searing images into the viewer's
consciousness without being followed by the announcer's
emollient comment, 'And now for something completely
different...' By the end of the evening, black horror has
paled into dull grey. And rightly so. A diet of unremitting
woe is not only indigestible but ultimately counterproduc-
tive. When horror becomes insupportable a merciful
numbing sensation steals over the human soul.

As for political extremism on television, even the statutory
fictional bigot like Alf Garnett is not permitted to get away
with his outrageous opinions without being humiliated in
the last act. The liberal viewpoint always triumphs as the
awful Alf gets his just deserts and slinks away like a
melodrama villain impotently threatening revenge. Beneath
all their bluster, the Alf Garnett figures of television are
revealed as cowards, ingrates and cheats.

It is hard to think of a single television programme on
offer, either factual or fiction, which communicates mean,
reactionary and destructive attitudes without signalling
quite clearly that these views do not represent the editorial
stance of the producer, department or television authority.

Programmes undoubtedly report that extremist convictions are abroad in the land. But even when samples are offered of the products of these ideological hate factories, editorial disapproval is always indicated by one means or another.

The strict truth is that the bigot, fanatic and extremist haven't an outside chance of an uncontested run on national television in Britain. The liberal ideology of television may be misty and vague but it effortlessly rules the ether. The decency barrier, vapid as it is, has proved impenetrable to the shock waves of extremism.

So the medium as minstrel is not in the business of being prophetic. Individual programmes may be prophetic in the sense of getting at the harsh truth behind the facts of a situation and showing the public things someone, usually in authority, would prefer they were unaware of. But overall, the medium nudges television-programme makers towards the centre of our culture. There the electronic bard is to be found celebrating our identity and affirming the things we hold in common.

We live at a time of great social fragmentation. W. B. Yeats's epigram hangs in the air over our society. 'Things fall apart; the centre cannot hold.' Yet the people search ceaselessly for a common cultural centre around which they can rally. Television has the power and will to provide one.

Those who make the claim that television, more than any other institution or influence of our time, is holding society together may seem to be overstating the case. But if television is not the most potent factor in creating such cultural consensus as exists at the present time, what is?

The Electronic Bard in Action
Let's see how television's bardic role works in practice. I take two popular BBC programmes from different areas of the output – sport and religion.

Sport is an activity where in ritual fashion artificially-contrived conflicts are resolved and harmony restored. Most forms of sport from football through snooker to sheep-dog trials have been successfully adapted for the small screen. Something over 20 per cent of the total output of British television is given over to sporting events.

The bardic function of television sport is illustrated by a programme such as 'Match of the Day'. The well-tried formula consists of edited excerpts from two of the weekend's football matches, presented by a resident expert in the studio, at the present time Jimmy Hill. There then follows a *melange* of interviews with players and managers and a 'Goal of the Month' competition. The cultural theme is about achievement through struggle controlled by sternly applied rules. That's a somewhat arid but accurate way of describing the game of football.

Watching 'Match of the Day' at home, the viewer has a dual role. He is highly partisan about the match, favouring one side or the other. But when the game is over and the play is analysed, he becomes a judge of form, skill and behaviour. Selected players and officials are paraded before him in the studio and he endorses or rejects their opinions.

The resident expert, Jimmy Hill, is expected to maintain an almost godlike objectivity, pronouncing on every aspect of the games from the technical quality of the play to the behaviour of the crowd. He moralises when players commit fouls, fans invade the pitch or the referee gives a controversial decision. Finally, he pronounces a verdict on the weekend's football as seen in the televised matches.

This is where the resident guru reflects the cultural consensus. He may appeal for better crowd behaviour or salute virtuoso football skills or protest at overcrowded fixture-lists and grossly inflated transfer fees. But his opinions are invariably drawn from the centre of the spectrum of public opinion rather than its extreme edges.

It is estimated that fifteen times as many people watch 'Match of the Day' as attend football grounds in person. Full weight must be given to human weakness; many prefer the comfort of a warm sitting-room to the rigours of a freezing cold football stand. But the mass attraction of the television version of the game may be partly due to the fact that the programme has more in common with a fairy-tale or acted-out fable than a 'real' football match. Hence, it appeals to a much broader spectrum of society than traditional sports fans.

Which brings us to the area of religion and that much lampooned programme 'Songs of Praise'. Christian congregations gather in some local church to sing well-known hymns chosen by a member of the community who is interviewed about his or her choice. The programme is hard to classify. It is plainly not worship, though recorded in a church, nor is it a factual account of some religious phenomenon or event such as a documentary film might offer. Yet millions of people watch 'Songs of Praise' who would never dream of attending church on Sundays.

Judging by the huge popular response to 'Songs of Praise', the electronic bard is obviously jogging some nerve and stirring up society's collective memory. Possibly the hymns recall key events in personal and national life, while the physical setting, a church, has all kinds of resonances for a people whose history and tradition are firmly rooted in the Christian faith.

It is unwise to dismiss, as the more captious critics do, 'Songs of Praise' as an orgy of nostalgia. Some of the interviews with Christians who have wrestled with crippling diseases, overcome appalling handicaps or are facing death buoyed by their personal faith are powerful and often disturbing pieces of testimony.

It is important that somewhere in our society traditional values should be affirmed, corporate identity reinforced and the robustness of folk religion celebrated. 'Songs of Praise' apes the Celtic bard in extolling the continuing power of tradition to help people face the future.

Critics may be right to accuse programmes like 'Songs of Praise' of being traditional, conformist and soft-centred. But that is like damning a porpoise for not being a shark or a bard for failing to be a prophet. Certainly, the programme emphasises comfort rather than conflict, plays up unity instead of division and extols the virtues of formal Christianity without dwelling over-much on its weaknesses. But this is television carrying out its bardic task of

articulating, affirming and orchestrating religious cele-
bration. It is someone else's job to set the people by the ears
and lacerate their consciences.

Moral Tutor
The very idea of television as a moral tutor will evoke a
hollow laugh from those who believe the medium unleashes
a tide of unwarranted sex and violence upon the ether. It
would be silly to ignore the many reports and books written
on this theme and well summarised by H. J. Eysenck and D.
K. B. Nias in *Sex, Violence and the Media* (Temple Smith,
1980). What emerges is a most complex picture from which
no simple moral can be drawn.

There is, however, one technical factor about television
which is not sufficiently taken into account when this
contentious issue of sex and violence is discussed by
moralists. Television does strange things when it portrays
human character and emotions. Being a crude medium it can
easily convey only a limited range of human expressions and
conflicts. I mean the word 'crude' literally. The grid of dots
by which television produces its image is located along 625
lines – which is a little like looking at the world through a
mosquito net.

This inescapable fuzziness of picture often forces television producers to favour images which are large rather
than small, simple rather than complex and obvious rather
than subtle. It is the sharper and more emphatic emotions
which register best on the screen. Hate, jealousy, violence
and aggression show up clearly while the more intimate
nuances of love, caring and friendship are blurred and
harder to delineate.

Simone Weil, one of the most luminous intelligences of
our time, wrote the following words almost a decade before
television began to attract huge audiences throughout the
world, but they are relevant to this subject:

> Nothing is so beautiful, nothing is so continually fresh and
> surprising, so full of sweet and perpetual ecstasy, as the good; no
> desert is so dreary, monotonous and boring as evil. But with

fantasy it's the other way round. Fictional good is boring and flat, while fictional evil is varied, intriguing, attractive and full of charm.[5]

So some moralists miss the point when they note that our television screens are awash with sex and violence and draw the conclusion that this is because television producers are depraved and wish to corrupt the public. The more mundane explanation is that the medium is technically suited to portraying the coarser human emotions and filters out the more subtle ones, just as a fly-net which captures an aerial bug will let the moonbeam through.

This line of reasoning is not offered to excuse the premeditated pornographer, but it should exculpate the honest television craftsman who tries to etch character finely as on glass and discovers that only the broader slashing cuts have come through.

There are artists abroad in the television industry who can capture on screen the whole gamut of human emotion from tenderness and intimacy to violence and rage. Others, having experienced the inherent resistance of the medium, give up the unequal struggle of working against it and settle for broad-band emotional content.

Of course, the television industry is sometimes afflicted with the disease endemic to mass-circulation newspapers – such treatment of a subject as will deliver large audiences at the expense of good taste. This uncomfortable truth the moralists have noted; the technical factor they tend not to take seriously.

The sex and violence issue is not off the point, but it is not primarily what I have in mind when I refer to the metaphor of television as a moral tutor. Nor was I thinking of the educational and information programmes television offers us.

The American scholar, Michael Novak, states bluntly that television shapes our souls.[6] The medium builds up in the viewer's mind, layer by layer, a structure of psychic expectation – which is what our years of schooling have done, but much more slowly. Television, he says, alters those parts of our psyche which have to do with perception, judgment, symbol and myth.

How does television go about the business of transforming the viewer's consciousness? He is taught new ways of seeing things, absorbs information differently, makes new connections between old ideas and is schooled in following a story-line like a circus tiger jumping through hoops to order.

Consider the pace at which information is doled out to viewers. In a television drama, the characters move briskly on camera, scene shifts are decisive and every line of dialogue is ruthlessly purged of dead spots, verbiage and awkward junctions.

The viewer also gets used to taking rapid changes of perspective in his stride. In the detective drama, for instance, the action may be taking place in three or four locations, each visited by the camera for a minute or less at a time, with changes rung hither and thither.

Following the story-line of a television drama, therefore, requires a form of multiple logic. This the viewer learns without the aid of traditional verbal signposts of the 'Meanwhile, in another part of the city . . .' variety such as are found in a book. With apparent ease, he works out the relationships between people and places paraded before him in bewildering sequence without the aid of a commentator or captions.

So television as the tutor of expectations trains the viewer to quicken the rhythm of his attention to the point where other forms of communication seem circuitous and slow. Traditional teaching methods relied on a painstaking advance of sequential logic, point being linked to point by careful exposition.

It would be absurd to suggest that television is the only source from which viewers derive their understanding of human nature. Each of us has, after all, some measure of self-insight and a wide range of relatives, friends, acquaintances and enemies who teach us plenty about human character by way of face-to-face contacts. Yet even the most gregarious of men and women find the gaps between generations, classes and races ever harder to bridge. So television's influence over our moral development grows as we make fewer real-life encounters.

Michael Novak as a university teacher is struck by the number of teenage students who, because their families have fragmented, admit to virtually no contact with or understanding of adults. Gone are the days when three generations gathered round the hearth, so that children learned how to rub along with parents and grandparents. Now most of the significant human encounters made by students are with contemporaries.

On their own admission, students rely on the mass media and chiefly on television to supply dramatic models of adult behaviour. Novak concludes:

> If it turns out to be true that television (along with other media like magazines and the cinema) now constitutes a major source of guidance for behaviour, to be placed in balance with what one learns from one's parents, from the churches, from one's communities and the like, then the range of dramatic materials on television has very serious consequences for the human psyche.[7]

Human behaviour patterns are, of course, remarkably diverse, but they tend to be formed and given shape by the power of available imaginative materials – stories, models, symbols and images. It is from this storehouse of the imagination that human beings draw models upon which to act in one situation or another.

When family and community ties are weakened, psychic development is atomised and there is no intermediate barrier between the human being and a national source of image-making such as television. Then the impact of the images on the screen is magnified because they are filling a psychic vacuum.

The immense power of television as a moral tutor cannot be ignored; moralists and teachers have got to operate through it if they hope to influence the contemporary person's development.

The Dream Factory

The operative word is 'factory'. There is a rather snobbish idea abroad that the television industry is a huge engine for the production and propagation of tidal waves of sensory garbage. This view is held most passionately by those who will insist upon drawing a false analogy between mass production in industry and in the mass media. Here a sociologist states the case:

> Much of what applies to the mass production of goods is also true of the mass media. We might be better off if newspapers were smaller, paperbacks fewer and television much reduced in quantity. In television, quantity has become more important than quality, and poor quality is concealed by dazzlingly effective presentation.

In one form or another this argument turns up all over the place, propounded chiefly by members of literary élites who feel the sheer volume of television output disqualifies the medium from being considered an art form. But the argument is fatally flawed because it combines a misunderstanding about television programme making with a misunderstanding about mass production.

First, the misunderstanding about mass production. Only in its very early days was industrial mass production limited to creating millions of copies of one or at most a handful of designs. Modern systems can produce endless copies of designs as numerous as the market requires.

Television is not a specialised application of industrial mass-production methods. The only thing 'mass' about television programmes is their distribution, not their manufacture.

In the sense that an identical product, a programme, is reproduced in millions of homes, television has a superficial resemblance to the making and distribution of, say, plastic cups. The difference is that each object (programme) is sculpted with immense care and great artistic skill. Though television producers hope their programmes will be widely watched, the same effort and ingenuity goes into an individual programme however small or large the expected audience. In any event, the producer does not know the size of his audience until after the programme has been transmitted, so he can't afford to take chances on shoddy workmanship.

Granted, the television programme, like the average article of industrial mass production, has a short life-span. It is shown on perhaps a couple of occasions and then vanishes for ever like a dream in the morning. But one ought not to use this argument to denigrate the cultural value of television.

Firstly, the rapid spread and the growing cheapness of home video-cassette recorders can offer television programmes a form of immortality. More importantly, there are certain cultural experiences whose very glory is in their ephemerality – for example, a particular performance of a particular musical work by a particular orchestra under a particular conductor. You can buy a recording but not relive the experience.

Those who work creatively within television have to come to terms with the dream-like evanescence of its programmes. They must balance short life against intensity of impact. Take the immensely powerful television drama about homelessness in Britain today, 'Cathy Come Home'. The programme may have been ephemeral in the sense that it was only transmitted two or three times. But its impact could not have been equalled had it been shown in a West End theatre for years on end.

Television drama is no longer a transplant from the live theatre. It has its own distinctive nature. The playwright who chooses to write for television is willing to forgo the longevity of theatrical performance for intensity of impact on the electronic screen. All who work creatively in television must accept this constraint.

So, dream factory? Television is a factory only in the sense that its plant is huge, complex and frantically busy. And it deals in dreams only to the extent that its programmes have a brief life-span. But the programmes are unlike dreams in their power to affect the destiny of society.

It is now generally accepted by historians, and confirmed

by President Richard Nixon, that television brought the Vietnam War to an end. The American people could not bear to watch on their television screens night after night news reports showing the suffering and death of their young men and the devastation caused to Vietnam and its people.

The Falklands campaign was mercifully brief. But given the horror of some of the news film, it is worth asking how the British public would have stood endless exposure to it had the fighting been protracted. I suspect that the pain and grief stirred up in the minds and hearts of the British people by the sight of British servicemen being maimed and killed in growing numbers would have wiped out overheated patriotic sentiments and forced the Government to seek a negotiated settlement.

An interesting sidelight on the Falklands campaign was the criticism heaped on both the BBC and the ITN for showing Argentine television film of the action seen through the eyes of the enemy. The moral is plain. Now the Age of Television has dawned, there will never again be one-sided news coverage of a war. This fact alone may make wars harder to sustain because the many-sided truth which must always be simplified or even suppressed to stir the people up for war will find its way on to television screens one way or another.

One need not succumb to the glamour of television, nor play down its ambiguous influence to acknowledge that one of the dreams the dream factory may help realise is that of a more tenacious peace.

TWO

Down the Rabbit Hole

The world of television is like Alice's Wonderland in two ways. It is packed with marvels and it has its own private system of logic. This is a curious blend of reality and illusion which reminds me of a snatch of repartee from *Through the Looking Glass* – 'Tweedledee said to Alice, "You won't make yourself a bit realer by crying..." Alice replied, "If I wasn't real, I shouldn't be able to cry!" "I hope you don't think those are real tears?" interrupted Tweedledum crossly.'

Appearance and Reality

We must start by taking a closer look at the television set in your living-room. Let me try describing it to the proverbial visitor from Mars – assuming his planet hasn't already scrapped TV as an antediluvian device.

The television receiver is a box with a screen on which cinema-like pictures appear. It also contains a speaker from which radio-like sounds issue. The viewer knows that it is not a radio because the words do not usually make sense without the pictures. He knows it is not the cinema because some of the pictures show things which are happening at that very moment.

The viewer recognises that neither the pictures nor the sounds originate in the box but come from somewhere else. His understanding is that the box is the means by which he receives into his home messages from the outside world.

These messages are broadly of two kinds – those which *present* events from the outside world and those which *represent* events in the outside world.[8] The first type of message is made up of pictures and sounds which convey to the viewer's screen such happenings as a news report, a sporting event, a political speech, a religious service or a current affairs documentary. The second type of message consists of pictures and sounds joined together in some acceptable artistic form to represent events in the outside world by means, for instance, of drama or comedy.

The viewer more or less accepts the convention that the kind of message which *presents* things is true and the kind of message which *represents* things is fiction. But this distinction is not actually very clear; the pictures and sounds themselves do not make it. This must be done by another message, usually from an announcer who signposts the category to which the original message belongs.

If this signposting is not done, confusion may result. For instance, in the 1930s, the opening sequence of a science fiction radio play, *The War of the Worlds*, was put across as a news bulletin announcing that the earth had been invaded from Mars. There was mass panic throughout the American city in which the radio station was located. The listener or viewer sometimes has no easy means of distinguishing between truth and fiction unless someone tells him.

Truth and fiction merge also because all the pictures and sounds, whatever their subject, have an artificial and therefore fictional quality. On the small screen, Neil Armstrong's moon landing does not look much different from a 'Star Trek' sequence. A multimillion-dollar space rocket and 200-dollar cardboard studio mock-up may seem to look equally real or artificial.

Nor do television production styles keep truth and fiction firmly apart. The drama documentary uses sequences in which actors play real people to tell a true story; or there is 'faction', which is a hybrid creature, equally classifiable as truth or fiction.

I must qualify this point. Television fiction seems different from lived reality most crucially in the matter of *pace*. Police do chase criminals in real life but not so many or so decisively as in fifty minutes of 'Starsky and Hutch'.

Ironically we often know that television is showing us real life because nothing much is happening.

The moon shots are a case in point. For hours, there is only 'more of the same' to be seen on the screen; certainly not enough action or character to be acceptable as drama. Television cameras covered the siege of the Iranian Embassy in London for hours on end; the action – the SAS assault – actually took a couple of minutes.

The viewer sometimes knows he has been watching the real thing when the pace is the rhythm of lived life rather than the accelerated momentum of fiction. But my main contention still holds – the boundary line between fact and fiction is vague, blurred and occasionally even indistinguishable unless someone tells us which is which.

The distinction between messages that are true and those that are fictional ceases to have much interest for some viewers who, provided they feel they can at least trust the news, are prepared to suspend judgment about the rest. So the messages come to be judged by a different standard from that of truth or fiction. The yardstick becomes credibility and interest. 'Is this programme believable?' (which is not the same thing as 'Is this true?') and, 'Is this programme interesting?' are the key questions.

The stock questions of the television producer, asked constantly in the studio or the film cutting-room are: 'Does this work?' 'Is it believable?' They are proper questions if not as high-minded as inner dialogue about truth and lie. If the veritable 22-carat fact is put across in such a way that it is not believable, the viewer will receive it as fiction.

Hence, in television, the metaphysical criteria of truth and untruth are replaced by aesthetic ones concerned with credibility and incredibility, fascination and boredom. The viewer boils down all the theorising to a single question: Is this programme worth watching?

Understandably, it is not the television producers sending the messages who are real to the viewer but the performers who speak them. Television personalities have a unique form of charisma. Many are famous quite simply for being well known. Their fame rests upon their celebrity, which in turn makes them even better known, and so on and on in an upward spiral of acclaim.

Even the most famous of the personalities parading before the viewer with messages are the creatures of those who send the messages. These stars will be obliterated from the screen without compunction if some change of style is thought necessary to intensify the messages' impact. Giving the viewer pleasure by being a well-loved and familiar face is no guarantee of screen survival. The TV personality only exists to serve the message, whatever it may be.

The television set has buttons which allow viewers to change from one channel to another. This confers upon them a sense of freedom and of physical control over what is going on. The choice is largely illusory because each channel is transmitting similar messages, though possibly in a different sequence. So the effect of television upon viewers' behaviour patterns is likely to be multiplied rather than neutralised when they move around between channels.

There is always the switch, of course. But for many viewers, to turn off the set is to undergo a little death. It curtails one of the few acts of communication between themselves and the world upon which they spend significant amounts of time.

The screen of a television set is not a flat surface like a cinema screen but a form of eye or window. It is not intended to provide a show or spectacle but offer a view and a vision. The screen is a window through which can be glimpsed things too distant or too near, too large or too small, too lasting or too ephemeral, too slow or too quick to come within the range of the conventional window. Just like Alice's looking-glass in fact.

Telly-Speak
Wonderland has its own private language. Let's call it telly-speak. It is to be found in its purest form in television commercials. Before I examine this strange patois, some thoughts are in order about television's impact on the traditional form of language and the literary élites who have for centuries dominated it.

The rise of a new form of mass communication such as television does not mean the obliteration of others which preceded it. People don't stop reading books or listening to the radio because their life increasingly centres on television. The media still coexist, but their relationship changes when a new arrival begins to dominate.

Television may have mortally wounded the cinema, but feature films are still an essential ingredient in television programme schedules. Most of the products of the Hollywood dream factories are now custom-built for the box in the corner rather than the local Odeon. Book publishing has not been wiped out by the television revolution, but an increasing proportion of books published relate to or augment television programmes.

A glance at the current bestseller list in the *Sunday Times* shows that four out of the six most popular hard-cover books are based on television series. And six out of the ten top-selling paperbacks are either biographies of television stars or literary versions of television dramas or comedies.

Paradoxically, television can inject new life into the faltering sales of some books. Evelyn Waugh's *Brideshead Revisited* and Vera Brittain's *Testament of Youth* are two examples of modern classics which were selling steadily but in modest numbers until they were televised, whereupon sales escalated dramatically.

What does happen is that the older media become parasitic upon the newly dominant one. Thus, an ever-growing proportion of column inches and pictures in the popular newspapers are given over to television topics, gossip about the stars and programme previews and reviews. Television besides being the central means of recording events is now generating many of the events in which the public is interested.

The argument that the society being shaped by television is moving back beyond Gutenberg, the invention of printing, to a total state of non-literacy must not be pushed too far. Spoken and written words still matter even though images convey the key messages of our culture. And for the first time in five hundred years, those groups and professions in society who live by mastery of the spoken and written word no longer dominate our culture though they still enjoy high prestige.

The ability to read and write has long been prized as the key to the treasures of knowledge and an essential qualification for social and cultural advancement. So, poor people made big sacrifices to give their children book-learning, and missionaries rated literacy as the most precious gift, after the Gospel, they carried with them to lands overseas. In effect, unfamiliarity with the alphabet reduced the majority of the world's population to the status of second-class citizens. Illiteracy became a synonym for ignorance in the cultured person's vocabulary.

From the Elizabethan Age, print-literacy has been the thing which above all else marked out the man of the world. He knew what was going on beyond the parish boundary, and because he could store experience by writing it down and refer to it at will, his opinions were rarely challenged by the people. He was also the custodian of proper speech patterns and linguistic usage. The way he spoke was correct; the way he wrote was grammatical. The dialects of the uneducated may have been rich in content but they were judged inferior to the extent they differed from the literary model.

It was inevitable that a culture transmitted from generation to generation through the medium of the printed word should be dominated by the literary élites – scholars, writers, preachers, lawyers, journalists and critics. As masters and mistresses of the medium they exercised a benign dictatorship.

Unlike the printed word, the meaning of television messages does not emerge in a linear fashion by a progression of ideas leading to a logical conclusion. The sense is to be found in a jumble and juxtaposition of mixed images, sometimes contrasting, often contradictory, and framed by words, music or silence.

The old literary élites, with a few exceptions, are not at ease in this new medium. Far from dominating things, they find it hard to get a hearing in the electronic market-place. They proclaim their opinions loudly, but few people seem to listen because the public is getting used to a quite different language.

Television programmes were originally judged according to the conventions of literary orthodoxy. It took some time for the truth to dawn that the rules of the game had changed. One might as well judge the pictures on the screen by the standards of oil-painting as impose the canons of literary taste upon television generally.

The language of Wonderland centred on the image rather than the word has a number of affinities with the old oral style of communication which the coming of writing displaced. Literary culture, for all its virtues, tends to dragoon the mind. Close-ranked regiments of printed text squeeze out rich if vague nuances of meaning and imaginative expression. Konstantin Stanislavski, the great drama teacher, made his students say 'Good-night!' in fifty different tones of voice. They could only *write* the phrase in one – dead-pan.

Television is able to restore shades of meaning which printed text excludes. In this sense, it shares with speech the richness and ambiguity of expression as against the neatness and clarity of the printed word.

Which brings us to telly-speak, the private language of Wonderland. Television commercials seem to be utterly vapid and unedifying. The message is hurled at us with a stridency that is ear-splitting. Those still securely rooted in literary culture resign themselves to the fact that they must endure commercials in order that worthwhile programmes can be paid for.

Because this is the received wisdom on the matter, it is not easy to convince most people that the television commercial is technically the most advanced use of the medium as a bearer of messages. The TV advertisement represents a whole new non-literary language, the complexity of whose structure is belied by the apparent simplicity of style.

It is an error to judge these utterly refined television messages by their verbal sophistication or lack of it. Words may strike deep but images strike deeper. That's what Freud meant when he said that thinking in pictures approximates more closely to unconscious processes than thinking in words.

Had Freud lived on into the Television Age he might claim that the television commercial, far from being a debased cultural form, speaks the language of the primal soul. Communicators who seek to address our society – preachers, teachers, evangelists and politicians – must take the genre with the utmost seriousness. That much-scorned television commercial does with ease what verbal pundits find so difficult in the modern world. It gets the message across without distortion or confusion.

The American historian, David Boorstin, Librarian of the US Congress, has no doubt about the central importance of advertising as a language of discourse in our society. He writes, 'If we consider democracy as a set of institutions which aim to make everything available to everybody, it would not be an overstatement to describe advertising as the characteristic rhetoric of democracy.' Jonathan Miller makes an even larger claim: 'The historians and archeologists will one day discover that the ads of our time are the richest and most faithful daily reflections that any society has ever made of its entire range of activities.'

Marshall McLuhan was truly prophetic about television commercials. As a university professor of English he might have been expected to share his colleagues' supercilious and dismissive attitude to all forms of advertising. Instead, he publicly proclaimed his enjoyment of them. They were not just cheery, colourful bits of filmic escapism designed to keep serious programmes apart and help to pay the television company's bills. They were icons, compressed images of a complex kind.

McLuhan's enthusiasm knew no bounds. Commercials, he claimed, are 'magnificent accumulations of material about the shared experience and feelings of the entire community.' The public agreed. Survey after survey has vindicated McLuhan's prediction that in time television viewers would cease to regard commercial breaks as infuriating interruptions of 'real' programmes. He said viewers would come to enjoy them for their own sake as brief but evocative works of television art, and more importantly, significant communications. He was right.

G. K. Chesterton said that every true story begins with a creation and ends with a last judgment. The television programme, whatever its form and subject – studio discussion, film documentary or live outside broadcast – is consciously shaped in narrative style to move from a gripping beginning to a decisive conclusion. Television is always an electronic story-teller; not just when it is dealing with fiction or news.

Hence, the TV commercial is the epitome of television style. It is a highly condensed story, much like a parable in being sharply observed, uncluttered with superfluous detail and aimed at spurring its hearers to action. Its unspoken pay-off line is strictly Biblical – 'Go, and do thou likewise!'

The compressed story-line of the commercial is carried sometimes by images, sometimes by the words, more often by a combination of both. The language is utterly contemporary and pellucid, without an underemployed syllable. The story hangs together, there is no confusion or distortion in it, and it is told with intense conviction.

Like the columns of the *Christian Science Monitor*, whose proud boast used to be that it printed only the good news, the television commercial offers built-in happiness. It weaves together images redolent of health, beauty and affluence to dramatise the good life. And the linchpin which holds together these individual symbols of happiness is the product being advertised.

We see a beautiful blonde, sitting in an opulent car, surrounded by muscular admirers, under a brilliant sunny sky, against the backdrop of a blue lagoon. And we are given to understand that this outburst of hedonism is sparked off by the bottle of amber liquid these beautiful people hold in their hands – Coca-Cola. This lightning tour of Paradise is given to us in just thirty seconds.

So powerful is Coca-Cola's advertising machine and so endlessly repetitive its commercials that there are whole stretches of the world where the very term 'Coca-Cola' has become a code word for 'the American way of life'. The sight of the brand name on a hoarding in Africa or Asia calls to mind not just a beverage but the life-style of the citizens of God's Own Country who are assumed to spend their lives lying on beaches, drinking Coca-Cola in the company of beautiful blondes.

Television advertising speaks to deep, though some would say not very admirable, human needs. One is the longing for happiness and the expectation that material possessions can provide it or at least fill the yawning pit left by its absence.

The desire to be among the élite who actually own what others are denied also offers a powerful motive for responding to commercials. Research shows that the viewers who most enjoy a particular television commercial are those who already own the product. Its value is enhanced for them because grandiose claims about its merits are constantly seen on the small screen.

The TV commercial exults in and happily exploits cliché and repetitiveness, qualities thought to be grave defects of style in the literary world. The commercial is not in the business of being original. So those purists who judge it by conventional intellectual standards tend to underestimate its power.

Commercials are visual statements dispensing conventional wisdom and seeking to evoke in the viewer familiar sounds and sights. They have much in common with the folklore of pre-literate peoples. Folk-songs and folk-tales are loved and valued because they have been endlessly repeated from time immemorial.

Children often cannot remember a time when they did not know the words of a well-loved nursery rhyme or jingle. The history of folk-tales not only stretches back into the misty past of one people, but often seems to leap-frog cultures. The very point of folklore is that it seems always to have been around.

That is the feeling the TV commercial hopes to evoke by way of a paradox. It proclaims the unique appeal of a particular product and yet at the same time tries to convince the viewer the product is an essential element in everyday life – as all-pervasive as the air.

Television commercials are very persuasive because the visual image speaks the language of affirmation. Pictures are hard to deny. It is not so difficult to say 'No' verbally because words are neutral symbols; they don't look like the bits of reality they represent. Pictures have great power. It takes a considerable act of will to resist them and disbelieve what they show.

Anthropologists have collected fascinating evidence about the power of visual imagery to get a positive response from pre-literate peoples even when the intention of the pictures is the precise opposite. There is no reason to assume that literate Westerners are any less suggestible.

Edmund Carpenter offers proof from his work as an anthropologist in the Western Pacific that people who think visually find it hard to say 'No' to what is seen. Here are two among a number of instances he describes.[9]

The Government of Papua New Guinea, anxious to protect Birdwing butterflies, issued posters showing pictures of the species with a warning that anyone caught with one in his possession would be fined ten pounds. District Officers were inundated by villagers bringing along specimens of the Birdwing butterfly, hoping to collect ten pounds a time.

The London Missionary Society fared little better when it launched a poster campaign aimed at curbing beer-drinking. Determined to make the message as simple and as vivid as possible, the missionaries designed a poster which showed a can of beer with the word 'No!' printed across it. Not only did beer sales generally increase but bartenders reported a great demand for a brand of beer called 'NO' they didn't stock.

Possibly the most insidious effect of TV commercials is that they blur the viewer's ability to distinguish between truth and fiction and so their impact lingers on throughout the rest of the programme output.

Public service broadcasting authorities who rule that the number of commercial breaks every hour shall be limited to, say, four, each to be of not more than two minutes' duration, are making one stark but highly dubious assumption. They think the viewer can suspend and reinstate his perception of

reality at will. Or put more simply, that he can switch at
great speed between taking in fact, absorbing fiction and
back again.

Consider an imaginary ten-minute segment of programmes to which the viewer might well be exposed
whenever he switches on his television set. He watches the
end of a 'true' documentary which is immediately followed
by a commercial. This commercial is both fact and fiction in
the sense that the story-line has been invented, but within the
fictional framework claims are made for the product which
by law must be true. Then the next programme begins. And
this happens to be a drama documentary in which actors
playing real-life personalities re-enact a historical incident,
but the script has been composed by a professional writer.
After that, a news-bulletin follows.

My point is that the rapid interplay between truth and
fiction must blur the viewer's apperceptions and take the
sharp edge off his discriminatory faculty. He cannot adjust
his mental monitor quickly enough to cope with this
succession of images fired at him at great speed.

It is this perceptual blurring which causes the messages of
the commercials to spill over into the rest of the output.
Viewers cannot be expected to react positively to an
advertisement for, say, Ford motor cars and then be
unaffected when the same make of motor car features
prominently in a drama or adventure film.

All in all, the television commercial is a highly structured
art form which really works as a way of changing people's
buying habits and therefore their behaviour. It is worth the
closest study by communicators seeking to address a post-
literate society.

The denizens of Wonderland who have mastered both the
language and logic of the medium are a new breed of
technocrat-artists.

The Young Turks

When BBC Television was resurrected after the Second
World War most of the administrative and engineering staff
were drawn from radio. The programme makers gravitated

into television from other areas of society which employed comparable skills – the theatre, journalism, light entertainment, publishing, the Church and universities. They were transplanted into television but never totally lost their original allegiance to their old professions and avocations.

The appointment of Alasdair Milne as Director-General of the BBC in August 1982 was, therefore, a landmark. He is the first Chief Executive of the BBC who has spent the whole of his career in television. He is the first of the Young Turks to become Pasha.

Whereas the first generation of television programme makers were old-type specialists in light entertainment, science, religion and so on, the Young Turks are able to operate across the board. They are classified by their command of technical skills rather than programme subjects.

Having been trained to use film or video, operate in studios or outside broadcast units, many Young Turks can move effortlessly from science to music and arts, from current affairs to sport. Some inevitably stay put in one department and in this sense specialise, but more give a fair impression of being modern Renaissance men and women – immensely versatile in their interests and knowledge.

This nomad-like wandering across the range of television programmes produces some interesting effects, especially in the religious departments of the various television companies. In the old days, it could be assumed that most of the staff of a religious department were Christian believers, many of them clergymen. Now the young professionals have moved in. Their convictions reflect those of society at large, so only a minority are likely to be orthodox believers in any faith.

These Young Turks find religion a fascinating area of human experience and approach it with a scepticism that is bracing. But some have the same kind of problem in understanding religious behaviour as a person staring through the glass of an aquarium trying to make complete sense of what is going on inside. It is hard to fathom the inner dynamics of marine life unless you get into the water.

Believers of the more traditional sort, outraged by so-called religious programmes they feel are destructive of faith and subversive of the Church, would, judging by the tone of their letters, apply, if they were able, some confessional test to programme makers in religious television. Only believers, they claim, are qualified to make religious programmes.

There are two obvious responses to this demand. Believers with the necessary technical skills are to be cherished, but they are in short supply in television. And the astringent approach to programme making of the Young Turks is an essential ingredient in public service broadcasting, whose organisations are barred by law from being propagandist in either a political or a religious sense.

There was a day when religious programmes were viewed with a certain fond tolerance by television controllers and exempted from the rigorous professional standards which applied throughout the rest of the television service. No longer.

In a time of fierce competition between BBC and ITV, television controllers will not trust big money to departments offering sub-standard programmes. The Young Turks by their professionalism ensure there is a uniformly high technical standard of programming right across the output.

Who are these Young Turks? What Identikit profile can be offered of this highly motivated and very influential television élite? Well, they are very bright, well educated and almost always middle class in origin. They have known no great wars (at least in Britain, which had no Vietnam) and precious little economic hardship. At the most senior levels, few of them are women and none is black.

The Young Turks squirt a sort of culturally homogenising mist over television because of their experience in the moulding presses of public school and Oxbridge. This does not make them any less committed or fiercely professional; simply more uniform in mind-set.

Stephen Hearst, former Controller of the BBC's Forward Planning Group, one of the most percipient television theorists of our time, has commented that the BBC and ITV attracted after the Second World War young men and women who in former times might have looked for a career in the Colonial Service. Alas, the British Empire inconveniently disintegrated before they could volunteer to serve it. And since they had a curiously British prejudice against careers in industry and business, they plumped for public service broadcasting as the nearest thing to a traditional vocation on offer.

Because television is a world of high technology, those who control it are in the top income brackets and enjoy much expense-account living because they must travel far and fast – though never *very* far from where the power centres are. They receive much respectful attention from a gawping world. The very mention of their trade opens most locked doors and has the usually inaccessible mandarins of public life welcoming them and clearing engagement diaries to fit in with television's requirements.

Television is a medium which inculcates a taste for power. It short-circuits the customary class and status barriers, bringing media persons of modest rank into intimate contact with the great and the good of wider society.

Many of the Young Turks of television entertain the notion that they are somewhat anti-Establishment in a very civilised and amused kind of way. To the ranks of the traditional working classes, they *are* the Establishment, more potent than public servants, of higher prestige than politicians and more exciting than the citizens of the world of academia.

Television is arguably the most powerful shop-window in the history of the world for enabling the educated to display their wares to everyone else. The more cynical observers claim that television just projects the fantasies of intellectuals about the way the rest of society lives and loves and dies.

The intellectuals of television have a vested interest in exploring new moralities and challenging traditional values, if only because the excitement of transgressing inhibitions and breaching taboos makes such gripping television. They do this in a liberal and tentative spirit, without heat, malice or extremism.

It is doubtful if most of the new élite realise what enormous moral stakes they are playing for, or consciously register that they are operating a kind of social control in the very business of making programme choices and selecting styles of treatment.

The Young Turks are the most powerful preachers of our time. They command audiences counted in millions and hold them in rapt attention. But they differ from traditional preachers in one regard – they would insist that they have no philosophy nor value system to communicate. Their only commitment is to excellence. That is a splendid aesthetic virtue, but it can render them non-combatants in the battle for the soul of our society in the Television Age.

THREE

Giant Footprints and Cable Stitching

Until the last few years the frontiers of Wonderland were bounded by the television studio, transmitter and viewer's homes. In the past decade however, a whole galaxy of new technology has been produced to increase the range and multiply the variety of television signals. High above our heads and deep beneath our feet communications filaments are spreading to bind the whole globe together as one gigantic television audience.

Star in the East

Early in 1982, the British Home Secretary announced that within four years the BBC would be given two satellite broadcasting channels; three more are to be assigned later to complete Britain's entitlement of five satellite channels. Even as he spoke in the House of Commons, the early generations of satellites shone like little stars twenty-three thousand miles above his head. Just as a Star in the East once signalled a decisive change in humanity's fortunes, now a whole forest of winking heavenly lights portends another.

Satellites are able to beam with consummate ease a television signal to any point on the surface of the globe. The artificial star which twinkles high above London at this moment will be appearing over the remotest parts of the Gobi Desert in the flicker of an eye. Now, it is not only God who is equidistant from every human heart.

Things are now moving so rapidly in the fields of satellite and cable-television technology that it is hopeless my trying to be topical. You must rely on the newspapers for that.

Instead, I want to concern myself with what all this will do to people.

One satellite stationed high over the Equator in the middle of the Atlantic Ocean can provide the whole of Europe and North America with all the two-way telephone, television and computer-data channels likely to be needed for the rest of this century. Put aloft two more satellites strategically placed and the entire globe can be served. Beneath the electronic footprints of these tiny giants the whole world can be welded together for the first time in history to form one gigantic television audience.

The original meaning of the word 'ecumenical' was 'that which pertains to the whole inhabited earth'. Then the ecclesiastical diplomats took the term over and domesticated it to refer to relations between Churches. Television may be the unlikely area of human endeavour which first gives practical effect to ecumenicism on a global scale.

To hook us up to the rest of the world, cheap ways have to be found of increasing the power output of satellites. The ordinary television set must also be modified to pick up signals directly from the air without the need for a costly ground station to amplify and pass them along. Scientists know how to solve both sets of problems; those in the sky and those on the ground. Everyone now waits for the techno-logists and industrialists to market the necessary equipment at an economic price.

The more affluent members of the human race can already buy dish antennae which when fitted to their television receivers will enable them to make contact with satellite transmitters.

Attacking the other area of problem, the BBC has taken the first step to cutting out vastly expensive ground stations by developing a mobile ground satellite terminal which is a three-metre dish antenna mounted on a trailer. The trailer houses all the necessary equipment to produce high-quality transmissions from a satellite signal.

There is something symbolic about the fact that this BBC portable ground station was used for the very first time to televise a service of worship from Ebenezer Methodist

Church in St Peter Port, Guernsey, in November 1981.

Hitherto, the Channel Islands have been beyond the range of normal outside broadcasts because of the high cost. The terrestrial line had to cross France and make several more hops before being routed back to the British Isles via the Eurovision link. The St Peter Port satellite broadcast was considerably cheaper and produced pictures of higher quality than a terrestrial link could offer.

So the technical problems of satellite broadcasting to domestic households are within an ace of being solved. What no one seems to be able to sort out is the snake's nest of political and legal issues that communications satellites have dumped into mankind's lap. These have to do with the human consequences of television ecumenicism.

The most urgent need is for some binding international agreement about outer space and what goes on there. This necessary advance has been held up because of the piecemeal way the various nations have handled the growth of satellite technology.

Within every country which is capable of creating satellite technology there are powerful lobbies demanding a share in deciding policy. There are the scientists who make the whole thing possible, the industrialists who produce and market the equipment and the chief consumers – the telecommunications, broadcasting, navigational, meteorological and data-processing industries. Then there are the overarching national and security interests which are carefully monitored by politicians, lawyers and the military services.

And behind the phalanx of interested parties there lurk in the shadows the ideologues who ponder ways in which these marvellous new devices for making nonsense of frontiers and overleaping Iron and Bamboo Curtains may be used to further the cause, whatever that may be.

Some countries have set up special government agencies to be responsible for the goings-on in outer space, others have just added to the responsibilities of existing institutions such as the Post Office or National Aerospace. Still others have been content to leave the whole thing, within limits, to private enterprise. Out of such national incoherence not

much international sense is likely to be made of the great
outer-space adventure.

As in so many other things, so also in this, the United
Nations Organisation shines forth like a good deed in a
naughty world. In 1967, after endless agonising, an Outer
Space Treaty was concluded whose primary aim was to
prevent military adventures among the stars. Outer space
was declared no man's land, or more correctly, everyman's
land. For the first time in a legally binding document, the
main contracting party is named not as this or that national
state but starkly and prophetically as mankind.

The committee appointed to work on the fine print of the
Treaty has been wrestling ever since with practical problems
such as the law relating to the rescue of astronauts, liability
in the event of a space disaster and the principles governing
the use of broadcast satellites.

The nub of the satellite issue is simple and challenging: it
has to do with the notion of the freedom to know. Is this
some kind of philosophical principle graven in the skies way
beyond any state's right to annul it if it wishes to keep its
citizens in ignorance about some things? Or is information
just as much a national possession as a uranium deposit or
parliamentary democracy or the Napoleonic Code or
apartheid?

If a nation has the right to decide which political and
economic system it will thrive or fail under, has it not also
the right to decide which communications system it will
adopt? Put more crudely and in the language of *real politik* –
have the nations with the technological muscle to launch
space satellites the right to use them to broadcast directly to
the people of other countries without the prior agreement of
the governments concerned?

Not surprisingly, the two states whose space technology is
most advanced are at odds on this issue – the Soviet Union is
in favour of international rules to govern satellite broadcasting while the United States is opposed to any legal
restrictions on the freedom of the airwaves.

In fact, some international regulation of satellite traffic is
inescapable. For technical reasons, satellites can only be

spaced every 4 degrees around the 360-degree circumference of the earth. Many of these, on station, would be poised over the oceans where the demand for their output is non-existent. So there is a fixed limit to the number of satellites able to operate without cancelling out each others' signals and creating a Babel in the sky. The scramble for what is available is bedevilled by all the old spectres of national prestige.

Just as many newly independent states, however poor and sparsely populated, regarded the setting-up of a national airline as an effectual sign that they had come of age in the community of nations, so most countries are insisting on their fair share of satellite orbital frequencies. They haven't the rockets to launch a satellite nor the television sets on the ground to receive its signals. Yet they believe that the radio and television frequency spectrum is a natural resource like the sun's rays or the rain which falls alike on the just and the unjust. It cannot be annexed by any single state or power bloc however mighty.

Questions to do with the ownership and right to use satellites for television broadcasts are only part of the problem. It is not only the method of transmission which is in contention; there are also key questions of content to be settled. Who decides what will be relayed from outer space?

Britain's honest documentary would be vile propaganda to the Soviet Union. What is light entertainment in Europe could be highly offensive to the Saudi Arabians. High-powered television evangelism may be quite acceptable in the United States but thought tasteless in the United Kingdom. What the Japanese consider art may be judged pornographic in Eastern Europe. So television by satellite lacks not only a legal framework to govern its operations but a cultural consensus to evolve rules for what is acceptable programming.

It is a fine idealistic thought that in a variant of the BBC's motto – 'Nation shall speak peace unto Nation' – countries might be able to offer one another their cultural riches through the agency of satellite television. The reality is dismal. Thus far, television has been about one group of nations speaking to the rest of the world which has no means of answering back.

Five years ago, a UNESCO report on world patterns of television flow noted that the United States imports less than 1 per cent of the programmes shown on its various television networks. On the other hand, between 60 and 90 per cent of the television programmes transmitted in the developing world are bought from the West, predominantly from the United States.

The reasons for the imbalance are obvious. Television began as a spin-off from the motion picture and radio industries. The West had a head start both technically and in terms of sheer quantity of output. There is also a very direct relationship between a country's wealth and the size of its domestic television market and therefore its ability to offer programmes for export very cheaply – the home market having already paid for the main costs.

Most important of all, television is a highly marketable commodity. Hence, the flow of material follows the general pattern of market trends, which is from rich nations to poor ones and from the Western and Eastern blocs to the developing world. Political imperialism may be on the wane, but cultural imperialism flourishes.

Third-world nations who have difficulty feeding their people usually cannot afford to buy satellite space. Any poor country that made the effort to use a satellite in order to reach a population scattered over a vast land area would have to forgo the luxury of international transmissions – domestic needs come first.

What Western television offers the rest of the world is, at best, without equal, and at worst, of abysmal cultural content. Either way, the ethos is Western because the programmes were made for our domestic market. So the alarming prospect looms of the cultural homogenisation of the world on the basis of a pallid Westernity.

Television traffic at present is running up a one-way street. The liberal dream of the cross-fertilisation of ideas and values across the world by means of satellite television cannot survive the cold realities of the present international economic order.

The satellite issue is a rigorous test of the practicability of our idealism. If we cannot yet gain acceptance for the notion that all citizens of the world have right of access to the same information, we are a long, long way from being able to establish any form of world government.

The question of satellite television provides us with a nursery slope on which to practise true internationalism on a realisable scale. When we get that right we can then attempt the commanding heights of world unity which are at present noble impossibilities.

Cow-Dung Technology

There are some inveterate television haters who rejoice in the fact that electronic gadgetry is so costly that with any luck vast stretches of the earth's surface will be preserved indefinitely from the scourge of television.

It will surely be a long time before the bushman of the Kalahari (per capita income two rabbits and a hyena's jawbone, shall we say?) can afford the simplest television receiver let alone the fancy antenna needed to pick up satellite signals. So poverty if not physical remoteness ought to ensure that for some years yet the only environment which enfolds people like the bushmen will be the one God gave them at the Creation.

This is a vain hope. These optimists, if that is the correct description for them, have obviously never heard of the redoubtable Professor Victor Papanek, nor of the remarkable SITE experiment carried out in India five years ago. First, the professor.

Professor Victor Papanek is a UNESCO international design expert and Dean of the School of Design at the California Institute of Arts. He has also taught at Purdue University in Indiana, USA, where he specialised in designing cheap equipment to be manufactured and used in the Third World.

The professor and his students designed a non-electric, thermocoupled cow-dung-powered radio for use in Indonesia, selling for less than 10p in 1971. With the increasing

availability of ever-cheaper materials it is quite likely that by
now the Government of Indonesia could afford to give these
sets away free at derisory cost to itself.

UNESCO set Professor Papanek and his students the task
of designing a very cheap educational TV set which could be
made in Africa of native materials and using local labour.

In doing the basic research for this set, Papanek made
some startling discoveries.[10] Television receivers manufactured in the technologically advanced nations such as
Germany had selectors for thirteen different channels, even
though there were at that time only two stations. So the
design team left out the expensive selector altogether since
the set would be operating on one channel only.

They also noted that a television tube's effective life was
severely shortened by the constant use of the on-off switch, so
this was omitted. The set would always be 'on', with current
drain being reduced to negligible amounts by the employment of transistors.

A major problem faced by all manufacturers who ship
their goods to Africa and Asia is that of insects fouling up the
insides of the machinery. These insects usually get into
television sets through the vents needed to prevent internal
heat build-up. All vents, airholes and fans were eliminated
from Papanek's design and any heat generated by the
operation of the set was drained off by burying an
aluminium heat sink in the casing round it. The shell of the
set was made of ABS resin and could either be mass produced
in a factory or manufactured individually by a single worker
in his own home.

The design team had to take account of a bewildering
array of scientific subjects and fields to ensure that every
possible snag was accounted for – climatology, anthropo-
logy, electronics and electrics, population densities, linguis-
tics, terrain (for transmission reasons) and religious and
social attitudes. In the end a set was designed which could be
made in Africa with African labour and materials for £2 (at
1970 prices).

In the light of technical innovations such as these, I would
not give too much for the chances of that Kalahari bushman

remaining for ever beyond the range of television's electronic ju-ju which can separate spirit from flesh more dramatically than his own magic rites.

If 'cow-dung' technology can provide people in the Third World with very cheap but serviceable television sets, how long will it be before they can also take advantage of satellite transmissions? Satellite broadcasting offers great benefits to the inhabitants of vast countries like some of those in Africa or on the Indian subcontinent where the distances are greater than conventional transmitters can cope with.

An important experiment was carried out in India in 1975. It was a prophetic sign of the shape of things to come in the Third World.

At 6.20 p.m. on August 1st, 1975, television tubes in over two thousand of the remotest villages in India lit up. The SITE (Satellite Instructional Television Experiment) project had begun. Each village had only one set and over two thousand people watched each.

None of these viewers had ever seen a television picture before, 95 per cent had not read a newspaper or seen a movie and over half had never heard radio. They were being exposed for the first time to the most powerful and unsettling of mass media. For a year they received each evening one and a half hours of news and educational programmes, all by courtesy of a huge ATS-6 satellite borrowed from the United States Government and relocated to include India in its 'footprint'.

The costs of SITE were remarkably low. Leaving aside the ATS-6 which was on free loan, the experiment cost the Indian Government ten million pounds. Indian engineers used great ingenuity to design receivers that could be built locally for much less than imported ones. They made the receiving antennae out of chicken-wire and front-end converters (used to transform the satellite signals into wave forms the television receivers could handle) for less than £100. The total cost for a village installation which would transmit a beautifully sharp picture direct from the satellite was about £400.

Each hour's broadcasting cost around £1,200 which

included both making the programmes and transmitting them. This worked out at something like 50p per hour for each set or .1p for each viewer. The satellite was, of course, only feeding around two thousand sets though it had the capacity to service many times that number. With the benefit of economies of scale the cost to each viewer could have been reduced to a minute amount.

The official report of the SITE experiment concluded that satellite television was not beyond the means and capabilities of most low-technology countries, and major projects have been launched in Samoa, the Ivory Coast, Niger, El Salvador and Mexico. Fifty other Third World countries use satellite television in one form or another. So neither poverty nor physical remoteness is likely to protect anyone on the earth's surface from the television revolution indefinitely.

There are immense political and cultural implications in bringing Third World peoples into the Television Age in one giant leap. When the electronic media hit a pre-literate people, excitability and restlessness are generated.

It is highly frustrating to receive mind-stirring signals and be unable to answer back. This tension is accompanied by a sense of expectation that there are even greater wonders to come. The institutions of a pre-industrial society are blown apart by the cultural and political pressures generated by the media.

I was in Zambia shortly after the first African nationalist organisation was founded. It is no accident that this happened around the time national network radio was established throughout the country. Radio had the effect of turning tribes-people into individual citizens long before there were political and administrative structures through which their citizenship could be expressed. This was a dangerously unstable condition. And if that is radio's impact, then the advent of television has even more volcanic consequences.

The spread of satellite television is bound to have an analogous effect to the arrival of network radio in Zambia. It will give viewers in diverse places a sense of being part of one world culturally, long before there are political and administrative structures through which that citizenship can be expressed.

Western Christians are alive to the effects of our economic policies on the developing world. We are also quick to condemn any remaining evidences of Western imperialism. But that pretty twinkling artificial star high in the heavens is potentially the most fearsome conquistador of all. And hardly anybody knows it.

Cable-Stitching

If satellite transmissions will enable us to become citizens of the world, cable television anchors us ever more securely in our own neighbourhood. Besides being the key to community broadcasting, cable is the essential element which links the television receiver to other electronic devices such as the computer, word processor and telephone. It is, therefore, at the very heart of the electronic revolution.

Yet the idea is hardly new. As long ago as the end of the nineteenth century, rich London householders could hear productions from major West End theatres in their parlours by means of a wire service and in the 1930s there was a well-established system of cable or relay radio.

British cable television proper began in 1949 as a way of solving the problem of poor reception in locations such as the shadow of high-rise flats or the lee of hills. A large antenna having been erected clear of the obstruction, the signal was piped into the affected homes.

By 1973 over two million homes in the United Kingdom relied on some form of cable or relay for their television reception. On the other side of the Atlantic, cable is becoming the standard means of transmitting television signals. In Canada, for instance, more than 60 per cent of homes get their television by cable. Throughout the United States the exact figure is disputed but reckoned to be around 40 per cent.

Cable began as a pragmatic solution to a technical problem, but has blossomed into a genuine television innovation. There is now the possibility of offering the viewer immediately dozens of television channels for very little cost and in a little while computer print-outs, data retrieval and two-way voice communication.

The experts describe the amazing capacity of modern cable this way. For voice transmission of reasonable quality a band of 10 kilohertz is needed – the telephone can carry one such conversation at a time. A present generation satellite can cope with 700,000 conversations, but the new fibre optic cable, which is very slender, offers a capacity of 30 billion conversations or signals.

Even the more primitive coaxial cable widely used at present can easily carry 24 channels of television. In 1972, the Post Office's Television Advisory Committee reported that the entire British Isles could be linked together by such a system of 24-channel cable television for a cost of £1,000 million. The Government of the day thought that sum prohibitive.

Now, the present Government seems to have woken up to the immense political and cultural significance and power of such a network. Our community is about to be cable-stitched together.

Cable television offers both bane and blessing. Everything depends on whose finger presses the button. It can break the stranglehold of remote network television professionals in favour of the local amateur, giving him or her access to the television screens of the community with programmes about grass-roots issues.

This democratisation of the ether is possible because once the basic network has been installed, cable television is very cheap to operate. No well-heeled commercial sponsor or big advertising interest is required to pay the bills. Private citizens can finance programmes if they have enough dedication.

On the other hand, the first contractor to provide cable television in any community is almost certain to have a monopoly because viewers are unlikely to subscribe to more than one service. So a cable service monopoly offers a power base of immense political significance, for as Abraham Lincoln wrote, 'He who moulds public sentiment goes deeper than he who enacts statutes or pronounces decision.'

The present network television, such as the BBC provides, deals best with the broad sweep of political issues whereas community cable television can offer detailed treatment of matters which preoccupy local voters. The state of the drains in Bermondsey or Wigan has no great appeal to the nation but it could be a gripping subject for the local cable station and its subscribers.

And because television confers fame and status on those who catch the camera's eye, the local politician or community leader who hasn't a hope of network exposure is vested with a new if somewhat circumscribed glamour. This is no bad thing because local government is as vital as it is usually dull. It could do with a touch of star-dust.

But good or evil consequences can flow equally from every human achievement. Cable promises local creativity, but also much scope for mischief.

If 'They' want to divide a community along racial or class lines, it is not difficult to wire black suburbs to receive different programmes from those enjoyed in white areas. Or shocking truths likely to stir up discontent or fan expectations among the poor can be excluded from transmissions to the shanty town section of the cable circuit.

Television can function as a window on the world showing the disadvantaged what might be theirs, sometime, somehow. Under malevolent control it may be made to operate like a mirror in which they see only distorted or false images of themselves.

Lord Reith, the founding father of the BBC, had a terse dictum which encapsulated both the scope and quality of good broadcasting – 'The best of everything for all.' So – slapstick comedy *and* music, science features *and* drama, religion *and* sport, current affairs *and* music hall variety, children's programmes *and* grand opera. And this catholicity of choice should be for all, not just those who can afford to pay for special services.

This Reithian tradition which grew up in radio has been carried over into television. The viewer who is prepared to go wherever the programme planners will take him for an hour or two is almost certain to find something to his taste. And

some of his most valuable discoveries will be made by
inadvertence or serendipity – the happy accident of
switching on the wrong channel or the right channel at the
wrong time and looking in on some programme he had
never thought to watch.

Many systems of cable television render such serendipity
impossible by offering totally predictable and often single-
subject programming. In the United States there are
channels which day and night pump out feature films, sport,
blue movies or religious services.

Thus, a cable monopoly can become downright perni-
cious unless the viewer has some recourse to network
television to redress the balance. Fibre optics cable may
permit us to link up with a whole Aladdin's cave of
electronic wizardry. It could equally well form a conduit for
surging tides of tastelessness.

The news in the summer of 1982 that the British
Government was setting up the Hunt Commission to make
proposals for establishing a cable system sparked off a fierce
debate about television standards and taste and competi-
tiveness. The two public service broadcasting authorities,
the BBC and IBA, whose affairs are regulated by Royal
Charter and Act of Parliament respectively, argued that there
must also be statutory control over cable operators if
standards were not to fall dramatically.

The line taken by the BBC in its evidence to the Hunt
Commission offered a fascinating insight into the thinking
and motivations of those who hold sway in Wonderland and
determine what its inhabitants will be able to see through
their magic windows. A fascinating mélange of attitudes was
revealed – a powerful drive for programme excellence, deep
distrust of big business and a faint tincture of elitism of the
'We know what's best for the public' variety.

The BBC supported by the IBA argued strongly that
statutory regulation had from the beginnings of broadcasting in 1922 provided a protective framework within
which a public service system could develop which was
committed to the Reithian concepts of programme excellence, enrichment of listener choice and widespread access to

the medium.

These regulations had a number of important consequences in the formative years of public service broadcasting. They shielded the BBC from the impact of the raw
forces of the market because the Corporation was not in
direct competition with other bodies for the same source of
funds. So the whole range of BBC programmes and services
could be budgeted on their merits and not exclusively in
terms of their popular appeal.

And the fact that such regulations existed forced upon
broadcasters and successive governments a continuing
dialogue about the social consequences of technical
advances in radio and television. As early as 1928, the
Postmaster-General was challenging the managers of the
BBC to demonstrate that their desire to increase the number
and power of relay stations would not disrupt the peace of
the whole community.

The broadcasters insisted that electronic technology was
so powerful and immediate in its consequences, it ought no
more to be exempt from regulation than road traffic or
nuclear fission.

Regulations, judiciously applied, had helped educate
public taste by laying down ground rules about decency and
propriety with a special concern for children and minorities.
So programme producers who were not naturally inclined to
exercise editorial and ethical discrimination were reminded
through such rules of the moral and social consequences of
their work.

The advantages of statutory regulation of all forms of
broadcasting were shown in 1955 when the Independent
Television system was created, and the forces of the market,
through advertising, were allowed a direct role in broadcasting for the first time. So firmly had the BBC established
standards of excellence that ITV had no option but to live up
to them. There is surely a moral here, argued the BBC, about
the best way to expand cable television services without
undermining the standard of public service broadcasting.

The BBC evidence concluded, 'If cable becomes symbolic
of what Mayfair can have but Brixton cannot, what

Metropolitan Man may enjoy but Rural Man is denied, then
one more social tension will be generated in an uneasy Age.'

In the event the Hunt Commission plumped for a system
of minimal regulation of cable by an authority independent
of either the BBC or the IBA. It also ruled that the cable
channels must carry BBC and ITV network programmes as
well as their own material. The new system was to pay for
itself by advertising – which did not please commercial
television companies who saw their own revenues being
decimated. Finally, cable television was to be denied
exclusive rights to the great sporting events which have
become part of the national birthright.

There *is* a whiff of elitism about the attitudes of the
relatively few broadcasting executives who up to the present
have determined what their fellow inhabitants of Wonderland may watch and listen to. They would retort that it is
because of their fierce professionalism and jealous attention
to excellence that Britain enjoys the finest public broadcasting system in the world. They greatly fear erosion
through a form of consumer elitism based on economic
privilege. They echo a question about cable systems posed by
the Aspen Institute: 'Will the new, serving the few, accelerate
the decline of the old, which were meant to serve the many?'

Whether the cable systems Britain will enjoy or endure in
the next few years are good, bad or indifferent, to judge them
primarily as channels of television is to have too short-
sighted a perspective. Their ultimate purpose is to provide
the infrastructure for a computer-related communications
network. The Electronic Cottage Industry is nigh.

D.I.Y. Television
One remarkable commercial success at a time of deep
economic recession has been the sale of domestic video-
recorders. It is estimated that one in every five homes in the
United Kingdom is already equipped with some form of
television playback machine. Robert Rowland, Controller
of Management Development at the BBC, characterises their
rapid spread in this way:

It took a hundred years for the telephone to reach 75 per cent of British homes. By comparison, it took twenty-six years for radio to reach 75 per cent of homes, seventeen years for television, fourteen years for colour television. If VCRs continue to spread, they could reach 75 per cent of homes within ten years.[11]

The video cassette and the device already being developed as its successor, the video disc, have been called 'a protest against rationed television'. They indicate that the viewers' appetite for television is unsated even by four network stations grinding out programmes for fifteen hours a day. And they signal the advent of D.I.Y. television scheduling as viewers decide for themselves what they will watch, how often they will watch it and at what time of day.

No longer will network controllers exercise editorial control over television output, decreeing what the viewer is allowed to see and how the mix of programmes will work out. Long-standing conventions such as the watershed rule will become irrelevant. This says that programmes containing a considerable degree of sex or violence must not be screened before 9 p.m. when it is assumed small children are in bed. If a viewer wishes to see an X-rated film in the afternoon in the presence of his small children he now has, by courtesy of the video cassette, the freedom to do so.

The video cassette means the end of the ephemeral nature of the television image. Images can now be stored, indexed and replayed. For the first time since Gutenberg, the invention of the printing press, the book has a serious rival as a handy device for storing information in perpetuity.

The value of video systems for educational purposes has already been realised. Almost all British secondary schools have video recorders whose cassettes restore to the student some measure of control over the pace of learning – sequences can be replayed again and again until a point has been grasped.

Because the material on video cassettes has not necessarily been recorded off network television programmes – some have been tailor-made for the purpose – this has important consequences for the style and development of programmes generally. Network television programmes have to be made to fit a strictly enforced time-slot and must be complete in themselves because they will be followed by another programme about a quite different subject.

Programmes made exclusively for video cassette can, within limits, run to whatever length the subject demands. And because these programmes will be seen only by those with a special interest they can present abstruse, difficult or even boring if essential material. The cassette producer is not required to entertain the generality of viewers as he would be if he were making programmes for the network.

Then there is the growing role of the video cassette as the provider of electronic games of the Space Invaders type. In the United States where they collect such figures it is estimated that in 1982, three times as much money was spent on video games as was taken at the cinema box-office.

And beyond the video game is the dark shadow of the cassette being used to offer packaged experience to the viewer, what Alvin Toffler calls 'electronic pleasure-probing of the brain'. There will be cassettes constructed to engender whatever mood the viewer chooses to adopt – a swirl of pictures, designs, patterns and strobic effects to generate excitement, sensuality or inner peace.

The video cassette and disc seem to wrest control of the domestic television receiver out of the clutch of the big television companies and hand it back to the householder. No longer will the set only speak and light up at the behest of those who over the first twenty-five years of television have taken it for granted they know what is best for the public. Such emancipations are always exhilarating – and dangerous.

All in all, the television set fully equipped with video, cable and satellite facilities offers an alarming surrogate for community living. The citizen of the Television Age will be able to pop down the rabbit-hole into Wonderland without leaving his chair – for work, for sport, for entertainment and for education. The ultimate privatisation of life is not far away.

FOUR

The Words of the Prophets

Rip Van Winkle, you will recall, took a sip from a keg of grog in the Catskill Mountains, fell asleep and eventually awoke to find himself a tottering old man, and America independent. He slept through a revolution. Western society over the past half-century has exhibited this Rip Van Winkle effect. For the first two decades at least of the Television Age no-one seems to have noticed the significance of what was happening. Except for a handful of prophets.

Early Soothsayers
The first full-length book on television was published in 1931 when the pioneers had just managed to get a crude 60-line image with no clearly recognisable shape. So any prognostications by the book's author, Edgar Felix, were highly speculative. In the event he was a little shaky on the technical future of the medium, but sound about its economics.

It would never be possible, Felix declared, for a television picture definition to exceed 200 lines, which meant that a studio face-to-face discussion could be transmitted, but not a sporting event or a feature film. In fact, current British television has a definition of 625 lines and some European systems are even more finely tuned.

Felix's predictions on the way the then non-existent television industry would have to be financed were right on the mark – in a word, through advertising. He wrote, of course, out of the context of America's laissez-faire society. He showed no awareness of developments on the other side

of the Atlantic where the BBC and Government were
evolving a licence-fee system.

Four years later, in 1935, when television receivers were
being tested in laboratories but had not yet entered the home,
Rudolf Arnheim wrote an essay for *Intercine*, the Journal for
the National Institute for Educational Film. He called it, 'A
Forecast of Television'. It was a major work of prophecy, not
only forecasting that television would become the most
powerful of the mass media of communication but also
spelling out its likely social and cultural effects.

He warned that television when it became universally
available would pose a great threat to the viewer's personal
fulfilment by turning life into a spectator-sport and leading
to the cult of sensory stimulation for its own sake.

Rudolf Arnheim was a generation ahead of his time. His
Cassandra-like warnings about television must have seemed
like the ravings of a fevered man to a society still trying to
absorb the impact of radio.

By the 1960s, however, the novelty of television had worn
off, just as Arnheim had predicted. Society had come to take
television for granted. And enough people had been exposed
to it over sufficiently long periods for the first research data
about its social, moral and psychological effects to be
analysed. The results caused selective alarm.

Parents and teachers worried about the effect of television
on children; the churches worried about sex and violence in
programmes; politicians worried about bias in news and
current affairs; and psychiatrists worried about the hypnotic
effect on the human brain of sustained bombardment by
television's cathode-ray tube.

Businessmen, such as publishers and cinema proprietors,
whose products stood to be superseded by television, had
their worries too – chiefly about survival. And capitalists
who had not been far-sighted enough to buy into television
at the outset worried that they might never get a chance to
purchase 'a licence to print money' – to echo Lord
Thompson of Fleet's evocative image of the financial
rewards of commercial television.

While all the interest groups were busy worrying about

different aspects of television, Marshall McLuhan burst upon the scene and put the whole debate in an entirely new context. He insisted it was a waste of time agonising over the content of television programmes in isolation from any understanding of what the medium itself does to what is communicated.

Typically, McLuhan made his point in an aphorism. He claimed it was as futile to assess television's significance by studying its programmes as to judge the impact of the invention of printing by analysing the contents of the Gutenberg Bible.

Such peremptory comments did not endear McLuhan to the embattled moralists who believed themselves to be beating back waves of televisually-induced sex and violence. But the force of his rhetoric and the sheer excitement generated by his ideas were such that he made himself the key protagonist in a fierce debate about the nature of the medium. Whoever wanted to argue about television had to argue with McLuhan.

The *Playboy* Prophet

Marshall McLuhan was a Canadian educated at Cambridge, who moved into the field of communications by way of Medieval English. In the 1950s McLuhan founded, with the distinguished anthropologist Edmund Leach, the journal *Explorations* which, to quote its epigraph, was concerned with 'exploring the grammar of such languages as print, newspapers and television' and with 'revolutions in the packaging and distribution of ideas and feelings'.

In a book called *The Mechanical Bride* (1951) McLuhan analysed advertising and propaganda methods. He claimed the State, like a 'malign work of art', uses the media to control consumption and perpetuate divisions such as those between business and society, work and home, action and feeling and between men and women.

Understanding Media (1964) brought McLuhan international fame, turned him into a cult figure and brought down on his head an avalanche of academic criticism. He took elements in modern society ranging from radio and television to money and clothes and examined them as media, as bearers of messages and creators of environments. His division of media into 'hot' – low in audience participation – and 'cool' – requiring work to be done by the audience – was widely quoted. The terms became part of the cultural jargon of the 1960s.

McLuhan brushed aside academic research about television and became a preacher. He went into the highways and byways of society with his message – the byways not excluding *Playboy* magazine for which he wrote extensively. The idea of a soidisant scholar putting across his ideas in a girlie magazine commonly judged to be soft porn had the academic world grinding its teeth in fury and chagrin. McLuhan was undeterred.

His secular gospel offered a new doctrine of man and of redemption. Its theme was: You are being changed *and* your family *and* your social environment *and* every thought *and* every institution you take for granted. The electronic media are reshaping and restructuring every aspect of your personal and social life.

Television, he claimed, has become a major landmark in the evolution of human consciousness by its ability to combine image with sound and relay them simultaneously – an extension of man, he called it, echoing the very words of Rudolf Arnheim thirty years before. McLuhan offered no empirical proof of this structural modification of man's nature. It was a notion to be entertained rather than a hypothesis to be tested. Prophets have a habit of putting things this way.

The McLuhan thesis that every major innovation in the means of communication produces shock waves of personal and social change is incontestable. We all know *that* – it is a general truth about the effect of any important invention. A. N. Whitehead, whose scholarship unlike that of McLuhan was *never* questioned, wrote, 'The major advances in civilisation are processes that all but wreck the societies in which they occur.' But McLuhan, with the touch of a visionary and poet, said it much more vividly by invoking as a parable the story of Cadmus, King of Thebes.

Cadmus was the monarch who, according to legend, sowed dragons' teeth which sprang up as armed men. He is supposed to have introduced the phonetic alphabet to Greece. McLuhan weaves together these two themes with great effectiveness. Dragons' teeth symbolised the magical power of the priests in ancient society; armed men represented the more prosaic might of the generals.

It was the phonetic alphabet that sealed the doom of priestly cabals whose power had rested in their knowing all the endless individual symbols of pre-alphabetical writing. But anyone could learn the phonetic alphabet in a few hours, so knowledge became widely disseminated throughout society. And the invention of papyrus as a cheap, portable writing material in place of slabs of stone completed the task of de-mystifying the priests, thus ensuring the rise to power of the military caste.

The image of Cadmus lodges in the mind as a palpable if oversimplified truth. McLuhan had this way with history. The alphabet, he said, made possible cities, roads, armies and empires. The printing-press fostered nationalism, Protestantism and individualism. Now the electronic media are fusing the world into one consciousness, and human consciousness into a simultaneous blend of all the senses. We are recapturing the gossipy unity of primitive community in this TV global village. We are beginning to share a world-wide nervous system.

The old institutions of the print era take no account of this revolution in our perceptions, McLuhan claimed. Our education methods become increasingly irrelevant, our politics more parochial and our sense of historical time eroded because the last twenty-four hours and the past twenty-four millennia are equidistant from us through the television screen.

Indeed, McLuhan claimed that history began with writing and ends with television. Just as there can be no history when there is no linear time sense, so we are living in post-history now that everything which ever was in the world becomes simultaneously present to our consciousness.

Of course, it wasn't as simple as all that. These huge

historical institutions could not have rested like great
pyramids on the point of single inventions, however
revolutionary. So McLuhan should be read in a spirit of
healthy scepticism to prevent the blood from rushing to the
head.

McLuhan's metaphors had a habit of flying out of control
because he tended to drive them too hard.[12] Take his startling
idea that television is an extension of the sense of touch
because the television image is not a photograph but a
constantly changing contour of objects sketched by the
scanning finger of the cathode-ray tube. Because our eyes
pick up light *through* the screen rather than *on* it, there is, he
claimed, a quality of depth to the image more akin to
sculpture or an icon than to a painting or sketch.

Common sense tells us this is a highly dubious notion if
only because the business of apprehending the image on the
screen is still done visually – any idea of tracing the picture as
if by touch is highly abstract. In any case, the whole thing
happens so swiftly that the viewer has no time to be tactile in
his response, as though he were a connoisseur handling a
piece of sculpture. And yet one sees what McLuhan was
driving at. There is the ghost of a truth imprisoned within
the error.

Nor ought McLuhan's contention that television transforms the world into a global village to be taken too literally.
The essence of true village life is face-to-face contact between
inhabitants, a shared physical environment and moral
concerns limited to the community's capacity to cope with
them.

The image of electronic media as an external nervous
system by which all mankind are linked together is a giddy
metaphor, but pushed too far it becomes neurologically
absurd. McLuhan did elaborate this metaphor in such detail
that one of his most formidable critics, Jonathan Miller, has
invoked McLuhan's Catholicism and accused him of trying
single-handedly to restore the lost world-consensus of
Christendom.

McLuhan declared that the global nervous system of the
electronic media could reunite the culture which was

splintered when the medieval synthesis broke down. *And* with this novel twist. The forces of science unleashed by the Renaissance which destroyed Christendom also created the electronic media and they may restore unity to human society.

This is Miller's understanding of McLuhan's ideas and seems to be a case of his out-McLuhaning McLuhan in reading more into a metaphor than is justifiable. But it neatly demonstrates the excited, even extreme, reaction that McLuhan's ideas provoked.

At the very least McLuhan has made us look at the media in a new way and ponder their impact upon human nature and history. His great contribution to modern thought can be summarised in the kind of image that would appeal to him. He was the man who pointed at the window through which we watch the passing scene and forced us to register consciously that it is there. And its optical peculiarities distort everything we see through it.

In a famous *Playboy* interview in 1964, McLuhan described his motivation as follows:

> I'm making explorations. My books constitute the *process* rather than the completed product of discovery. I want to map new terrain rather than chart old landmarks. But I've never presented such explorations as revealed truth. As an investigator, I have no fixed point of view, no commitment to any theory – my own or anyone else's.

Marshall McLuhan died early in 1982 and a number of grudging obituaries suggest that old academic enmities still prevent an honest appraisal of his prophetic ideas. He was a curiously solitary figure on the landscape of communications history. That seminal work, *Understanding Media*, has not been built upon; it is a literary mule. But so was *Finnegan's Wake* and few scholars deny James Joyce's genius.

An Afterword
This rambling trip around the television world may serve to convince that it is a ludicrous understatement to describe

television as a communications *system* or an entertainment
medium or a leisure-time *pursuit.* Television generates its
own *cosmos,* a created order which is virtually an alternative
form of reality.

Karl Marx said that all historical events happen twice;
once as tragedy and again as comedy. Similarly, almost every
event in the contemporary world happens twice; once *out
there,* and again on the television screen. You will have your
own opinion as to which is comedy and which tragedy, but
without doubt a new duality has entered our lives.

Which version of an event is more compelling, what
appears on the screen or the real-life one? Millions of viewers
have actually decided this issue by choosing to watch
television for hours every day when they could be actors in
the tragedies and farces being played 'out there'.

I recently went to Lords to watch a test-match after years of
following cricket on television. Every time a wicket fell or
the umpire made a controversial decision, I half-expected to
see an instant-replay such as I would have got on television.
It was exasperating to be denied close-ups and slow-motion
repeats of the action.

If pressed, I suppose I would plump for the 'real event' –
atmosphere and all, but it's a close-run thing. It is not
frivolous to wonder which version of cricketing reality is the
more gripping.

Whether or not television is as *authentic* an experience as
real life, it is increasingly becoming the *authenticating*
experience. David Boorstin writes:

> The television experience is what makes an issue live, what
> makes a politician into a statesman, what makes or unmakes a
> President, what makes an event catastrophic, what makes a
> question controversial, what makes a far-off conflict momen-
> tous and what makes a neighbourhood event significant.[13]

Religious groups regularly lobby broadcasting authorities asking for their religious services to be televised just as
those of the mainstream Churches are. The leaders of these
sects and groups freely confess they have no expectation that
an occasional televised service will attract many viewers as

recruits to their cause. However, they feel it important that their own followers should have evidence that television takes them seriously. This is a variant of Descartes' dictum, 'I think therefore I am' – 'We have appeared on television and therefore we exist'.

Television is an alternative form of experience which puts a question-mark against all happenings that are not represented within its cosmos. Therefore, the quest for improving the quality of life now faces a new challenge, a double task. We must try to make things better not in one but in *two* worlds or parallel versions of reality – on and off the tube. For these two are independent variables.

Boorstin has adopted a term from ophthalmics to describe man's need to keep an eye on these two versions of experience. Our society, he claims, suffers from *diplopia* which is a vision disorder that causes objects to appear double.

If television forces us to develop *diplopia* in order to live at the intersection of two realities, how do we keep our bearings in the solid world? Indeed, given that increasing numbers of people devote more time each week to watching television than to doing anything else at all, what for them *is* the solid world?

That is a religious question. For one of the functions of religion is to help people to see the world as it really is. So we consider next what part religion plays in the alternative cosmos of television; how the medium deals with matters of faith. Beyond that question is a more intimidating one. What form ought effective Christian preaching and witness to take in a society being transformed by television?

A Commercial Break

There follows an interlude in which I offer some media parables, in no particular order and without comment. They are quotations, anecdotes and general snippets of information which have shed light for me on facets of the Mediaworld. I found all of them provocative.

*

'Oh what a beautiful baby!' exclaimed a visitor.

'That's nothing,' replied the mother, 'you should see his photograph!'

[Old Jewish joke]

*

In the 1970's the United States spent £200 million on the Apollo-Soyuz joint space link-up with the Soviet Union. When officials of the National Aeronautical and Space Administration were asked to describe the scientific and technical benefits of the mission, they admitted there was none. The whole thing was done, they said, to provide American viewers with a space spectacular 'more thrilling than *Star Trek*'.

*

A poor mother when asked why she was spending precious money to exchange her black and white television set for a colour receiver, replied, 'I don't want my children growing up not knowing what colour is.'

*

A women in an American TV studio game was offered a

prize of several thousand dollars if she would fire one round from an air rifle at a photograph of her son. She refused, and lost the money.

*

Of all the senses, trust only the sense of sight
[Aristotle, *Metaphysics*]

*

At stake ultimately in the difference between literature and television are the prerogatives of two moral universes, two cultures and two ideas of creation. Both forms, just by existing, pay tribute to their source, the power which makes them possible – literature to the Word, television to the Light. But beyond that, by implication when not directly, literature celebrates a God transcendent, television a God immanent; one affirms creation by fiat, the other creation by emanation.

[W. R. Robinson]

*

Oh, what a blow that phantom gave me!
[*Don Quixote*]
[Title of a book by Edmund Carpenter]

*

The first comic books came out in 1935. They caught on with the young. The elders of the tribe, who had never noticed that the ordinary newspaper was as frantic as a surrealist art exhibition, did not notice that comic books were as exotic as eighth-century icons. So, having noticed nothing about the *form*, they could discern nothing about the *contents* either. The mayhem and violence were all they noticed. They waited for violence to flood the world. Or alternatively, they attributed existing crime to the comics. The dimmest witted convict learned to plead, 'It wuz comic books what made me do it.'

[Marshall McLuhan]

*

Television? The word is half Latin and half Greek. No good
can come of it.
[C. P. Scott, legendary Editor of the *Manchester Guardian*]

*

Suppose a person, even an entire group is ignored by the
media? Until recently, America was full of 'invisibles'.
Blacks were ignored in literature. On radio, they became
Amos 'n Andy played by two white men. On film they
became comic servants. They were never shown as cowboys,
though in real life about a third of the post-Civil-War
cowhands were black. Deadwood Dick was black as coal, but
on film he turned pink-cheeked and blue-eyed.

Blacks made their first public appearance on TV when
they turned to violence. Suddenly they were no longer
invisible. For one brief moment, they could be seen on TV.
At which point, they were also seen on the streets.

But that moment passed quickly. The media image soon
shifted from real blacks – unemployed, uneducated, hungry
– to 'media blacks' – well-dressed, professionally employed,
college-educated. Real blacks once more became invisible.

[Edmund Carpenter]

*

The purpose of my remarks is to focus your attention on this
little group of men [sic] who [through TV] wield a free hand
in selecting, presenting and interpreting the great issues in
our nation. They decide what forty or fifty million
Americans will learn of today's events in the nation and
world. We cannot measure their power and influence by
traditional standards. The American people would rightly
not tolerate this concentration in government. Is it not fair
and relevant to question its concentration in the hands of a
tiny, enclosed fraternity of privileged men, elected by no one,
and enjoying a monopoly licensed and sanctioned by
government?

[Former US Vice President Spiro T. Agnew, 1969.]

*

Public opinion is necessarily moulded by a few large plain simple ideas.

[Sir John Seeley 1834-95]

*

A young Mexican-American hijacked a plane and offered to release his hostages in return for a 5-minute TV interview about the ill-treatment of his people. He kept his promise.

A man in Sacramento took hostage the employees of a bank so that a TV news team would report that neither he nor his father could get a job.

Lynette Fromme shot at President Ford, she claimed, so that when she was eventually interviewed on television she could warn America that big business was destroying the planet.

[Edmund Carpenter]

*

Fred Silverman's Ten Commandments for creating a popular TV programme. As President of NBC on a salary of a million dollars a year, he helped the Corporation to outstrip its rivals, CBS and ABS, in viewer-ratings:

1 Make people laugh. There's enough tragedy in the world.
2 Start off with a star.
3 Stress the positive, not the negative.
4 Glorify the common man.
5 Familiarity breeds acceptability; forget originality.
6 Cartoons aren't only for kids. Don't be too clever.
7 If you're going to take chances, take big ones.
8 Grab 'em when they're young.
9 Keep the plot moving – fast.
10 Hold 'em for the first 90 seconds and they're yours.

*

In 1971, according to the *New York Times*, the Pentagon proposed to President Richard Nixon that an electronic gadget be attached to every television set in the country. Capable of being activated directly by the President, it would switch all the sets on at the same time if there were a national emergency. After a heated debate, the proposal was dropped. For the time being.

*

There is a tribe in New Guinea which daydreamed about such things as gods and demons, significant places and important events in the tribe's life. They then illustrated these daydreams on beautifully worked masks. Each year the masks were burned so that the imagination could exercise its right to create living myths. The custom survived the advent of radio, but not television.

[Harvey Cox]

*

TV shows seethe with myths and heroes. They guide decisions, inform perception, provide examples of conduct. Does that make our mass-media culture 'religious'? I do not think we can explain its grip on people any other way.

The media's preachers tell us what our transgression is: our armpits are damp, our breath is foul, our wash is grey, our car is inadequate. They hold up models of saintly excellence before our eyes: happy, robust, sexually appreci-ated people who are free, adventurous, competitive and attractive. These blessed ones have been saved, or are on the way. And the sacramental means of grace that have lifted them from perdition are available to you and me - soaps, deodorants, clothes, pills, cars.

Mass media culture is a religion, and we rarely get out of its Temple.

[Harvey Cox]

*

There is a dangerous optimism which regards communi-cation as a quantitative proposition, forgetting that the crucial point is not to use the media, but to *change* them. What we need is not a rejection of these media but a critical use of them, a building up of our own criteria and style and a

struggle with their demonic culture-destroying tendencies.
[Heinrich Kraemer]

*

Newspapers were born free but television was born in chains, a monopoly created by the state, dependent upon the state and in every country regulated by the state.
[Sir William Rees-Mogg when Editor of *The Times*]

*

In August 1979, the 'Muppet Show' was removed from Turkish television during the month-long Ramadan fasting period. It was thought that 'Miss Piggy' would be offensive to devout Muslims who regard the eating of pork as unclean.

*

'The patriotic Archbishop of Canterbury found it advisable . . .'
'Found *what?*' said the Duck.
'Found *it*,' the Mouse replied rather crossly. 'Of course you know what "it" means.'
'I know what "it" means well enough when I find a thing,' said the Duck: 'It's generally a frog or a worm. The question is: what did the Archbishop find?'
[*Alice in Wonderland*]

*

When Abby Mann's film *Judgement at Nuremburg* was scheduled for transmission on American TV, the American Gas Association succeeded in having any mention of Nazi gas chambers removed from the script. And the American Florists' Association have threatened to remove their sponsorship of any drama serial in which bereaved characters talk about donations to charity being given in lieu of flowers.

*

I would not be surprised if, fifty years from now, almost no one will pay attention to paintings whose subjects remain *still* in their frames.

[André Girard]

*

For the first time the young are seeing history being made before it is censored by their elders.

[Margaret Mead]

PART TWO

GOD-IN-A-BOX

FIVE

Man in the Gap

Religious television raises a number of crucial questions which do not face the rest of the television output. It all starts with John Reith, the founding father of the BBC. His giant shadow lies across religious broadcasting to this very day. There are things done in the name of religious television which are only explicable by tracing them back to their roots in Reith's attitudes. What follows is not a potted history of religious broadcasting; merely a sketchy account of Reith's ideas and policies.[14]

Religious broadcasting in Britain was supremely Reith's creation. He moulded it, urged the reluctant Churches to take account of it and agonised over its effectiveness – 'I have been more anxious about the general religious policy of the BBC in matters great and small than about anything else,' he wrote to William Temple in 1930.

It was John Reith who persuaded the Revd A. J. Mayo, Rector of Whitechapel, to become the first-ever religious broadcaster by giving a Christmas Eve talk on the air in 1922. And it was Reith who the following year subjected the then Archbishop of Canterbury, Dr Randall Davidson, to his first experience of the wireless.

Anxious to convince the religious Establishment that radio could be a potent means of proclaiming the Gospel, Reith invited the Archbishop and his wife to supper and contrived to switch on the wireless set while they ate. The sound of Schubert's 'Marche Militaire' filled the room. Dr Davidson declared himself thunderstruck, while Mrs Davidson enquired whether it was necessary to leave windows open while the radio was on so that the wireless waves could get to the set.

The demonstration had its effect. The next day, Archbishop Davidson called a group of Roman Catholic, Anglican and Free Church leaders to his room at the House of Lords and formed what was first called the Sunday Committee and later the Central Religious Advisory Committee.

John Reith was a Scottish engineer, a son of the manse who was deeply devout in a no-nonsense kind of way. The epitome of good religion for him was his revered father; a close runner-up was one of the early religious broadcasters, Dick Sheppard, vicar of St Martin-in-the-Fields, whose faith Reith eulogised as 'thorough-going, optimistic and manly... unconcerned with the narrow interpretation of dogma and centred on the application of the teaching of Christ to everyday life'.

Reith believed fervently in divine guidance. One Sunday in October 1922, while he was between jobs, he went as usual to Regent Square Church where at the evening service Dr Ivor Roberton preached from a text in Ezekiel, 'Thus saith the Lord, I sought me a man to stand in the gap...' In his diary that night Reith noted, 'I still believe there is some great work for me to do in the world.'

A few days later, scanning the advertisements in the national press, Reith read that a company was about to be set up to engage in something called 'broadcasting' and needed a general manager. At his interview, one of the directors of the British Broadcasting Company assured him that this novel medium, wireless, was destined to become so central to British society that the general manager 'would soon know everyone worth knowing in the country'.

That was enough for Reith. Satisfied that the task was of heroic proportions, he took the job and privately ascribed his success to Providence. In his diary he commented, 'I had kept my faith alive; night and morning had comforted and encouraged myself with the words, "Commit thy way unto the Lord, trust also in Him and He shall bring it to pass".'

No chief executive of a broadcasting organisation with so vivid a sense of divine destiny could possibly have regarded religious broadcasting as a minor matter. Asa Briggs in his official history of the BBC comments that for Reith religion was the most important subject of all.

Certainly Reith chafed at the infuriating reluctance of the Churches to take advantage of his positive attitude to religious matters. He felt he was making the running in their stead. 'Why do not the religious authorities,' he complained, 'clamour for a place in the ether? It is high time they got to work and took proper and full advantage of the BBC attitude.'

In his earliest account of broadcasting, *Broadcast over Britain*, published in 1924, Reith described the avowed aim of the British Broadcasting Company as the attempt to bring the best of everything into the greatest possible number of homes. He railed against those who claimed his job was to 'entertain' them, using that word in so debased a sense that there was great danger of 'prostituting the powers of a great scientific invention and insulting the character and intelligence of the people'.

Holding to so elevated a doctrine, Reith looked to religion not only to purify the ether but also to permeate the broadcasting organisation. The nature of the output and of the institution must be of a comparable nobility. Hence, without apology, he admits to quizzing prospective employees about their religious beliefs – 'A man's philosophy of life, his attitude to religion, were as highly relevant in some departments of broadcasting as professional skill in others.'

Religious broadcasting had to be of central importance to a man who ran a broadcasting organisation like an enclosed religious order. Dick Sheppard described Reith as 'a man with an unshakable belief that righteousness alone exalteth a nation' and as 'a rock that shall not be moved'. There is a certain wintery undertone to those compliments, or at least a kind of steely quality is imputed to their subject. He was a hard man.

Reith was a thorough-going Sabbatarian. He viewed the

growing secularisation of Sunday in the 1920s with distaste. He wrote, 'The surrender of the principles of Sunday observance is fraught with danger even if the Sabbath were made for man.' He insisted that the true test of the BBC's effectiveness was not the extent to which it reflected the secularist tendencies of the age but the vigour with which it resisted them.

In the BBC's *Handbook* for 1928 it is baldly stated, 'The BBC is doing its best to prevent any decay of Christianity in a nominally Christian country' ... the *BBC*, note, not just its Religious Broadcasting Department. The whole organisation was enlisted in a crusade to hold back the forces of Anti-Christ threatening to engulf British society.

Sunday programmes had to be planned with the sacred significance of the day in mind. There were to be no transmissions during church-going hours unless a religious service was broadcast. On Sunday afternoons there were two hours of music and then a godly silence until eight-thirty at night when it was assumed that churches' evening services were over and the flock had safely returned home. Listeners were then treated to a short act of worship broadcast from a studio.

Sunday-night programmes ended with another Reithian innovation – the 'Epilogue' – though the credit for inventing the name of that programme beloved of comic parodists goes to B. E. Nichols who was London Station Manager at the time. It was said that the penultimate mark of an announcer's fall from grace – one stop short of dismissal – was when Reith refused to allow him to read the Epilogue.

Though John Reith was unyielding in his principles and fervent in his faith he was not a bigot. He defended his right to give the Christian religion prominence in his schedules with the declaration that 'Christianity happens to be the stated and official religion of the country; it is recognised by the Crown. This is a fact which those who have criticised our right to broadcast the Christian religion would do well to bear in mind ...' But he insisted that the Christianity which was broadcast should be 'unassociated with any particular creed or denomination'.

Reith was a pioneer ecumenist. From the very outset he insisted that the group of clergy who planned the studio acts of worship should include a Roman Catholic priest as well as a Free Church minister. Where else in the world were regular interdenominational services held as a matter of course in the 1920s? When Dick Sheppard agreed to conduct the first experimental broadcast service from St Martin-in-the-Fields in January 1924, Reith laid down only one condition – the liturgy must be 'undenominational'.

Traditional Christians worried that broadcast services of worship would lend themselves to widespread profanity – epitomised by the Dean of Westminster's immortal line about the appalling prospect of a man in a pub listening to radio worship with his hat on. A more reasonable fear of many church leaders was that congregations at Sunday worship might be seriously depleted. It was for this reason that the Dean and Chapter of St Paul's refused to allow a live transmission of Evensong from the Cathedral in 1926.

Reith dealt with what he regarded as ecclesiastical cold feet in his usual forthright manner:

> There has been an occasional expression of fear that by virtue of the broadcasting of religion in general and of complete services in particular, attendances in church would fall off. Even if this were so, the possibility of which I absolutely deny, and which we would all deplore, it is probably of small moment compared with the numbers who are now hearing what they would otherwise not hear.
>
> I think it is absurd to suggest that church-goers will surrender their habits of attendance for what is obviously a poor substitute. If the Churches recognise their new opportunity, there will not be room enough to hold their people.

Judged by the time and thought Reith gave to religious matters, one might imagine that religious broadcasting was a major element in the early BBC schedules. In fact, it occupied less than 1 per cent of the weekly transmission hours. But for Reith it was pivotal, and his expectations were staggeringly high. In language which even in the 1920s would be described as fulsome, he set the scene for Sunday broadcast worship:

> There is no telling the effect when, for this brief period in a busy
> week, the lamps are lit before the Lord, and the message and
> music of eternity move through the infinities of the ether, filling
> the whole earth with the glory of them, as once there appeared a
> glory in the cloud and a spirit moving upon the face of the
> waters.

Religious broadcasting would never have so absolute an
endorsement.

Reith had none of the doubts which were to assail later
practitioners of religious broadcasting about what they were
doing. Though in the 1930s the acids of modernity were
already leaching away the foundations of traditional
religious observance, the damage only became apparent at
the end of the Second World War. In Reith's view, any
reasonable listener ought to respond to broadcasting which
was rooted in a strong, mainstream religious tradition, put
across with sincerity, without frills or fussiness, and executed
with high professionalism.

Religious broadcasting was to be an adjunct to the work of
the Churches, not an attempt to supersede it. The aim was to
whet the appetite of the unbeliever, strengthen the faith of
the believer and offer aid and comfort to Christians unable to
get along to their local churches. For years, the opening
announcement of the weekly Evensong from Westminster
Abbey included the phrase, 'For the special benefit of the
sick'.

Though Reith was a passionate believer in religious
broadcasting, he was not indulgent about professional
standards. He and the Head of Religious Broadcasting
he appointed, Frederick Iremonger, afterwards Dean of
Lichfield, maintained a firm editorial control over broadcasters and programmes. Though the mainstream Churches
were encouraged to use the airwaves, it was made clear they
had no absolute right of access; they broadcast by invitation.
And some Churches and sects were excluded by deliberate
acts of editorial policy.

There was a fastidiousness about Reith's choice of ecclesiastical advisers, Iremonger, William Temple, Cyril Garbett and Dick Sheppard, which, combined with his Scottish hard-headedness, preserved him from the temptation of developing religious broadcasting along parallel lines to that on the other side of the Atlantic.

No superheated evangelism, no high-powered monetary appeals, no three-ring Gospel circuses found their way on to the air-waves so long as Reith was Director-General of the BBC. For him, religion could claim no exemption from the mandate he gave to broadcasting generally – it had to inform, educate and entertain.

The best of everything – that was the simple dictum Reith coined to encapsulate his broadcasting philosophy. The goal was to be excellence reached by professional skills in every part of broadcasting, including religion. He believed that whatsoever things are good must be enhanced when transmitted with integrity and skill.

Reith insisted that religion should not be indulged nor treated as a special category but judged according to general professional standards. This is his priceless legacy which has been handed on to this day. But the world in which the religious broadcasters must ply their trade has changed beyond recognition in the half-century since John Reith left the BBC to become chairman of Imperial Airways.

'Enthronements and Drumhead Services'
John Reith left the BBC in 1938 when television was still in the experimental stage, so he had no direct influence over its practical development. In the post-Second-World-War years when a BBC Television Service was being planned, there was a general feeling among professionals that religion was one of the subjects which would not transplant from radio to television.

In 1946, Dr James Welsh, a very distinguished Head of Religious Broadcasting, told the Central Religious Advisory Committee of the BBC that he did not see that religion could contribute much to television other than 'enthronements and drumhead services'.

The Churches were reluctant even to go so far as 'enthronements' and other state occasions on television. When the then Princess Elizabeth married the Duke of Edinburgh in 1947, the ecclesiastical authorities refused to allow television cameras into Westminster Abbey for the solemnisation, even though the processions and events outside it were fully covered. But with curious logic they agreed to the service being filmed. The film was then shown that night on television.

The Central Religious Advisory Committee was assured in 1948 that 'the fundamental religious policy of the BBC is the same for television as for sound broadcasting'. Hardly anyone at this time was asking McLuhan-type questions about the nature of the medium. Television was generally assumed to be 'radio with pictures', so it was taken for granted that the structure of the medium would *allow* the same policies as those which applied to radio.

All the old taboos which religious radio had to overcome were resurrected by the Churches in the early days of television. Only one religious service was televised before 1948 – a service of consecration of a war memorial chapel at Biggin Hill. Ecclesiastical observers invited to watch an experimental televised service in 1952 took the view that the faithful might find 'real' services boring after seeing snappy, showbiz versions on television, so dire warning notes were sounded.

The number of worship services televised increased from once a year in 1948 to once a month by 1955. There were two reasons why the frequency was not stepped up. The first was a shortage of Outside Broadcast units. The location of Sunday services had to coincide with important sporting fixtures taking place on the Saturday. Early religious television producers had graven on their hearts, or at least in their diaries, the dates of such events as the Lincoln Handicap, the Boat Race, the Cup Final and Wimbledon.

But there was a more fundamental reason for the restriction of the number of religious services televised, and this had to do with the theological reservations of the first Head of Religious Broadcasting of the television era, Canon

Roy McKay. He wrote:

> The shortage of OB facilities was sometimes very annoying, but I came to be grateful for it. It gave me the chance to weigh up what I wanted to do in television, and it was not long before I was clear that I did not want to overweight religious programmes with church services.[15]

McKay did not want general viewers to identify religion primarily with what goes on in churches, since it was becoming obvious the public were staying away from places of worship in ever greater numbers. But he had also cottoned on to some of the structural differences between radio and television. Ought the viewer to look in on TV worship as a spectator or was it possible for the television direction to contrive the impression that he was invisibly present in the congregation?

Neither option was attractive to McKay. If the viewer saw only what a member of the congregation actually present could, that must make for very dull television. If, on the other hand, the camera toured the church, pausing here and there, this was something the ordinary worshipper did not do and became voyeurism.

McKay decided that it was very difficult for the viewer to worship by way of television. This was where radio differed from television. Radio listeners could, if they chose, 'see' themselves as worshippers by using their imagination. But the camera held captive the television viewer's imagination.

Roy McKay's conclusion was perceptive, and had it been heeded a whole snake's nest of theological and technical difficulties might have been avoided:

> I think Christians should hesitate before committing themselves to the position that the televising of the ordinary service enables the viewer at home to share in the worship of the church. Even sympathy for the old and sick should not be allowed to fog our judgment of what Christianity demands of those who take part in public worship.[16]

In spite of Roy McKay's strictures, analogies between

radio and television continued to be drawn and whole areas of religious programming were duplicated. Once the Churches got over their initial suspicion of the new medium they came to expect the same privileged right of access to television they had enjoyed on radio from the beginning. The Central Religious Advisory Committee pronounced, 'No modification is required from television in the general principles on which programmes in sound only have been carried out.'

Colin Beale, the first full-time Religious Broadcasting Organiser in BBC television, insisted that television was different from radio. As early as 1953 he was warning against television's 'keeping too close to the Sound parallel'. He advocated the adventurous use of drama and film to exploit the visual nature of the medium. But, then, Beale came to television from the Churches Film Council and so was fluent in the language of the image.

Roy McKay and Colin Beale as prophetic pioneers in the field of religious television were calling attention to the un-radio-like properties of the medium before Marshall McLuhan's visionary ideas were common currency. But it was when the Young Turks, the first generation of television professionals, turned their attention to religion that the real theological issues were laid bare.

The Young Turks were not particularly interested in theological questions; they merely wanted to deploy the whole range of television techniques to an area of human experience which fascinated them. In so doing, they forced a reappraisal of what religious television is all about. Their cool professionalism made them unwitting agents of radical change.

SIX

Sacred Conundrum

John Reith was anxious to broadcast worship because it was, for him, the most significant thing Christians did together. He wanted the airwaves to carry the Gospel into every home. So the linchpin of religious broadcasting was the church service in one form or another. Around it were clustered other types of programme – discussion, talks, the occasional drama and sacred music – but worship was the paradigm of religious radio.

Throughout the history of radio there have been those who questioned whether it was possible to broadcast worship without changing its nature. They argued that so many of the conditions for true worship according to Christian tradition could not be fulfilled by the radio version, that it was stretching language to call it worship at all.

Television has added several layers of complexity to this problem. Radio listeners don't think they are physically present at a broadcast service. Only one sense plus their imagination is involved. They are still firmly anchored to their armchairs in real life. Television, however, creates the sense of an alternative reality. Can worship be incarnate in a ghost medium? Hence, the scepticism about whether it makes much sense to talk about TV 'worship'.

In the Television Age, if what is happening on the screen is, according to a rigorous theological understanding, truly Christian worship, this has important implications for the Church. If it is not worship, then the broadcasters need to think seriously about what they are doing and why they are doing it.

Whenever television worship is discussed seriously, religious broadcasters divide into two sharply contrasting groups with a number of bridge-builders, either more visionary or confused than the others, spanning the gap. Conservatives start from the premise that it is the worship of the gathered Christian community which is normative and every other form of activity so labelled (not excluding the television variety) is to some extent an unsatisfactory substitute for the real thing.

The radical view is that worship is a basic human activity which can be done in all sorts of ways and in many places; it certainly cannot be confined to the form and style associated with the historical Church. There is no reason why a form of worship expressed in the idiom of television cannot be evolved which would both engage Christians at home and viewers right outside the ambit of the Churches.

The conservative claims that what happens in so-called television worship fulfils very few of the requirements of 'true' worship as it has been understood throughout Christian history. It ought, therefore, to be an offence under the Trades' Descriptions Act to call it worship at all, except in the strictly descriptive sense – 'This morning's worship comes from St Gertrude's by the Gas Works'.

The more extreme radical also disposes of television worship, not by pronouncing it impossible but by insisting that the distinction between worship programmes and the rest of the religious output is a false one. If a programme evokes the feelings and attitudes associated with a fairly liberal definition of worship then that's good enough; it is wasted effort to argue about labels.

At root, this argument is not only about worship but also about the nature of television. The conservative is a one-cosmos person – there is a real world (where true worship takes place) and television can only partially represent what goes on in it. There are many things television cannot do, and worship is one of them.

The radical believes there are two cosmoses – the so-called real world, and then its mirror-image, television, which is an alternative form of reality. It offers a universally accessible experience which competes with the rest of our experience. Tele-culture is a real world which viewers inhabit, so they can worship with other viewers who are joined mystically with them within the environment of television.

To get this most crucial of all religious television issues into some sort of perspective, I shall spell out the conservative case, and counterpoint it with the sort of rejoinders a radical might make.

Worship is a team activity. Only *in extremis* ought it to be a solitary experience. So the lone viewer watching television is in an abnormal situation from the outset. Television does transmit programmes about team activities, for example, sporting events. But only in the case of worship is the proposal that the viewer sitting at home can be taking part in the same sense as the players on the field in, say, 'Match of the Day'. A keen footballer will want to watch 'Match of the Day', but he is fully aware that viewing is a different activity from kicking a ball around as a member of a team.

Worship is also about commitment. The person who is truly worshipping wants to bring his or her own life to God and not just look on while others do so instead. Nor is the impetus to commitment usually given in a vacuum; it issues from the life of a Christian fellowship.

Certainly viewers might in their desire to register commitment be moved to go along to a local church (which local church?) at the first opportunity, but the odds are against it once the moment of acute sensitivity has passed. Or they may resolve to make some act of commitment there and then. What do they do next? What device is there in a television act of worship to enable them to make connections with the formal community of faith?

Worship is a sacramental activity. By this is not meant that it should invariably involve the eucharistic rite, but that it is *corporeal*. All the senses of the whole person are engaged – things are handled and tasted and smelt as well as seen and heard. Television worship only recruits a viewer's eyes and ears, and even then, they are not connected in the same way as in real life. Other senses wander freely. Of course, the senses of worshippers in church may also wander. But they do have the option: they *can* be fully sensuously present. The television worshipper cannot.

This dislocation of the senses applies to all television, of course, and not just to its religious programmes. However, there are few if any other areas of television where the viewers are invited to undergo life-transforming experiences, especially when they are not present to the medium as whole people.

Worship is a counterpoint of opposites. Sounds and silence, movement and stillness, giving and receiving, corporate and individual responses – all are integral to true worship. Television worshippers get a lot of sound but little if any silence. They are still but never active, receive but cannot give and are alone but not one of a number. Hence, they get only half the experience, and this may be a case where half a loaf is not better than no bread.

The radical responds to this clutch of points by saying the sharp distinction drawn between the physical environment of a conventional worship area and the domestic TV watching area is based on outmoded presuppositions about science, theology and liturgy. It is Stonehenge religion to believe that individual people watching TV screens are separated because they are not simultaneously in one stone building.

The notion that television worshippers are isolated boils down to a psychological rather than physical problem. If worshippers feel isolated, it is because they do not *perceive* themselves to be part of the worshipping mass. That is up to them; the barrier is not of television's making.

The radical also insists that remote physical contact can be less real than spiritual communion. An act of worship, say, a broadcast of Choral Evensong heard on a car radio on a motorway may be a more intimate experience than rubbing shoulders with other shoulders in church. Indeed, in the vastness of some cathedrals where the choir is away in the far distance and half a dozen worshippers are scattered throughout the area of a football field, the worshipping location is more denuded of people than the motorway.

And what about the Communion of Saints? Surely, says

the radical, no Christian seriously doubts that we share worship with them even though we are denied physical contact?

The conservative might interject at this point that it is not *for choice* that fellowship with the Communion of Saints is strictly spiritual rather than corporeal. The operations of certain biological laws have rendered impossible what all Christians would surely desire. Television worshippers are choosing physical isolation plus spiritual communion by their own wish and this is irregular. The exceptions, of course, are Christians house-bound by reason of illness, age or other infirmity. They would be at church if they could. For them, television worship is a regrettable second best.

On a different front, the conservative worries about the doctrinal confusion likely to result from successive acts of worship televised from churches of different and often theologically contending denominations. The BBC and IBA justifiably pride themselves on their pioneering role in ecumenical worship, but the practical reality is that worshippers can only reach beyond a particular tradition provided they are securely within it. They are only free to explore the circumference if they are sure of the centre.

I refer to theological traditions, not to denominations. There are obviously non-denominational Christians about but there are no theologically neutral ones – the moment we own up to having any kind of dealings with Christ, we put ourselves in one theological tradition or another as we reflect on the nature of those dealings.

In a televised church service, viewers are given a weekly lucky dip into a variety of Christian traditions; in studio worship they are at the mercy of the ecumenical strengths and weaknesses of the producer. Either way, in so far as they associate themselves seriously with what is going on, they are making, week by week, affirmations that may be at odds with one another. The truth is that broadcasters cannot, over a run of weeks, serve up a theologically balanced diet. They can only try to achieve some crude kind of denominational spread.

So the onus is on viewers to find the one voice or voices

authentic for them in the midst of the clamour of the electronic Tower of Babel. Varieties of worship may strengthen the faith of a mature believer; they can be confusing or even destructive for someone whose nascent faith needs to be nourished by the discipline of regular exposure to a coherent but limited body of truth.

Worshippers need to believe a few things deeply before they are bombarded by a lot of things coming at them from many Christian traditions. So if TV is their only source of worship, they are in trouble.

It is true that very few viewers complain that they have developed theological vertigo as a result of watching a run of miscellaneous televised church services. This is probably because they do not really associate themselves so intensely with the individual and varying acts of worship that conflicting dogmatic affirmations jar.

To move freely from one of the theological mansions to another as an appreciative guest if not a resident requires considerable sophistication and spiritual maturity. The Churches themselves are not yet very adept at this kind of catholicity. One can hardly expect television viewers to respond to what they watch with a degree of theological sophistication the Churches themselves have thus far failed to achieve.

The radical thinks the conservative's anxiety on this score is the result of a confusion between liturgy and worship. Liturgy ('the work of the people') is by definition something that is done by Christians together and in a form which has evolved throughout the history of the Church. Worship is a basic human activity which can take many forms. It requires neither corporate physical action nor a set structure embodying formal theological statements that may get mixed up week by week.

Television cannot create liturgy, the radical concedes; merely observe it taking place in real-life communities. But the elements of a form of worship suited to television can be transmitted, using the idiom of the medium itself.

For instance, a sense of awe could well be engendered by a clip from David Attenborough's series, 'Life on Earth' or

Carl Sagan's 'Cosmos'. A scene from 'Coronation Street' might evoke joy and a news-bulletin film report drive viewers to their knees in contrition or intercession. And the whole might well be given shape, not using the traditional categories of Christian liturgy but within the framework of, say, those Jungian archetypes which are supposed to be the most elemental images found in our unconscious.

All this would be very costly because of copyright problems and the effort of sifting through the miles of film and videotape used on television every week. But the radical claims it would be a genuine television experience using the special codes of the medium which the habitual viewer has become accustomed to.

The target audience for such an enterprise would be very different from that usually associated with television worship. Research shows that outside broadcasts of worship services are watched for the most part by Christians hors de combat by reason of age, infirmity and so on. They are likely to find such a radical restatement of television worship exasperating because it would *not* remind them of what is happening in the local churches they are unable to attend.

On the other hand, television viewers who are right outside the Church's circle of influence might well find worship in the television idiom congenial to them. It would not confront them with an experience they have consciously rejected nor would they fear being enticed back into the formal community of faith – which is an implicit evangelical assumption of much traditional television worship.

Equally significant, such radical television worship would not necessarily be Christian in symbolism or intention. Its producers could well draw their visual material from many sources, not excluding any of the great faiths. The aim would be primal worship – to sensitise the viewer to the deep mysteries of existence that underlie and swirl through all higher religions.

Advocates of radical television worship quote some interesting proof-texts to support their case, such as the writings of humanist thinkers who affirm the value of worship as a secular or at least non-theistic activity. Sir Julian Huxley, for instance, acknowledged the value of worship not as 'grovelling before a Supreme Ruler', but as 'an opportunity for a proclaiming of belief in certain spiritual values, for refreshment of spirit ... for expressing in music or liturgy various natural religious emotions of praise, contrition, awe and inspiration, which would otherwise remain without adequate effect.'[17]

The humanist philosopher, R. W. Hepburn, also rates worship highly as a 'celebrating of moral perfection and beauty, fused in an intensifying strangeness ... worship is not the preface to a life of submission to commands from without: it is rather the extension of the scope of moral judgments and moral vision.'

Whatever may be thought about such a view of worship, it cannot be denied that it would have the advantage of being truly catholic in the sense that devotees of some religions other than Christianity could take part without sacrifice of integrity. This would dispose of one of the more divisive effects of full-blooded televised Christian worship – it excludes Jews, Muslims, Sikhs and Hindus. These are significant communities of licence-fee payers who have the right to expect their ultimate concerns to be reflected on television.

It is a highly contentious issue whether television worship expressed in such symbolic Esperanto is worth the candle when there are as yet no universalist religious communities in contemporary society with whom the viewer can link up. The conservative is dubious of the value of any form of worship which does not issue in service and is not based on a coherent system of belief. Those radicals who are Christians insist they have no desire to sell short the Christian faith or the Churches. They advocate primal worship because they believe this is as far as television can go in accommodating the activity.

Advocates of the radical position on television worship are willing to settle for a strictly spiritual fellowship among viewers, so they need not concern themselves with a number of technical problems facing the conservative trying to bring televised worship as close to its 'real-life' equivalent as the medium will allow. The worship programme transmitted from a television studio and the outside broadcast of a church service offer different but formidable hurdles for the producer to surmount.

First, worship from a studio. To most viewers, the television studio is the place of unreality par excellence. Most of the activities they associate with studios do not take place in the real world – panel games, discussions, musical spectaculars, comedies – and so they are not required to suspend disbelief. They accept the studio as a glossy fantasy world created for their entertainment. At this point, the radical might suggest that whether studios are 'unreal' or not is debatable. The average viewer is probably more familiar with the inside of a studio than the interior of a church.

The studio is the place of high professionalism. Viewers have been taught to expect the very best of entertaining skills. They will accept a mediocre guitar-playing vocalist in an outside broadcast from a church because within the convention of a happening in real life most guitar-playing vocalists *are* amateurs. But viewers expect the best in a studio, and usually get it. Hence, in that context, amateurism comes across as incompetence and spontaneous items 'feel' unplanned and are therefore unnerving. This goes for all the performing skills.

On the other hand, if every performer is highly expert, the activity has lost that 'randomness' characteristic of a truly worshipping community, where some members of the congregation sing out of tune, the organist plays false notes, children drop hymn books and the sermon is punctuated by Mrs Blogg's hacking cough. A congregation is casually composed, not highly selected. High professionalism tends towards theatricality in the studio, just as amateurism can be embarrassing.

Because outside broadcast units are vastly expensive and in great demand to cover a multitude of sporting activities, producers of religious programmes find themselves having to make more and more use of studios for worship programmes. So the question, 'Is this "real" worship?' is raised in an acute form.

An outside broadcast of a church service is taking place in real life - if the cameras were not there it would still go on - but the studio operation exists solely for the purposes of television. It stands or falls on whether or not the viewers *can take part*. If they cannot, the whole business is futile because the studio operation, unlike a televised church service, has no other *raison d'être*.

The very presence of television cameras at a church service must affect what happens. The viewer's perspective is different from that of a physically present worshipper because someone else - a television director - is choosing what will be seen and experienced. No real-life worshipper would spend so much time gazing up the nostrils of fellow worshippers as the cameras do.

The key problem of televised church services is exquisitely simple - and insoluble. Television is a visual medium, but the object of worship, God, is by definition, invisible. He is not accessible to cameras and microphones.

Nowhere else in television does it happen that the star of the show is off-camera altogether. The parallel would be a comedy show in which the cameras spent the whole time watching the audience laughing rather than showing the comedian, or a sports programme where what was happening on the field could only be captured as reflected in the expressions of the spectators.

Worship is directed at God - the congregation is schooled to put aside all egotism and self-reference and concentrate on the Almighty. The television cameras, however, have only the congregation to keep in view, apart from the architectural setting. So the worshippers must be shown singing, praying, listening to a sermon and generally being engaged. This stands the thrust of true worship on its head, making the worshippers the focus of attention rather than the one who is being worshipped.

The radical asks why viewers should be interested in watching other people worship. Into which of Reith's three categories does such electronic voyeurism fall – is it entertaining, enlightening or educational? If none of the three, why do it?

For viewers who switch on their television sets casually, an outside broadcast of a church service makes sense because it is a specific instance of the general rule that television eavesdrops on most areas and activities of life. And if they are Christians *hors de combat* they probably know how to integrate what is happening on the screen into their spiritual life.

But ought religious television to be in the business of offering an emergency service for sick saints? The question needs to be asked not simply for reasons of broadcasting philosophy but on theological or even Biblical grounds. Whose job is it to care for aged and sick Christians? The New Testament is clear about this. The local community of faith must see to it that members who are laid low and unable to meet for worship receive the means of grace. Religious television neither can nor ought to do the work of the local church for it.

The more conservative religious television producer greatly fears the creation of a substitute Church which has no existence except in the airwaves. If there are significant numbers of viewers who are open to the claims of religion as presented on television and nowhere else, ought this vicarious discipleship to be encouraged? And how can its pastoral dimensions be accommodated by the television authorities who are in the business of making and transmitting programmes and not running a counselling service?

If television can only transmit an attenuated version of Christian worship, to what extent is it able to fulfil the functions of a Church for viewers whose only link with religion is through the small screen? Even if it is possible to relate viewers to God by means of television, there is no mechanism for relating them to each other. And this is surely one of the key things the Church is all about – loving and being loved, forgiving and being forgiven in the setting of face-to-face encounter.

Public service broadcasting organisations such as the BBC and the IBA have neither the mandate nor the means to provide a pastoral after-care service for viewers of television worship. In which case, who can? Possibly the Churches could. Yet there would be endless complications in putting enquiring viewers in touch with particular congregations because of denominational divisions. Television worship assumes a degree of practical Christian unity that does not at present exist.

So, ought worship to be transmitted at all? 'Of course, it should!' retorts the radical. 'But without attempting to use the model of the gathered Christian community and its activity as a paradigm. And without being doctrinaire about categories of religious programmes.' Away with the damning label 'worship'! Let's stop agonising over the technical problems. The issue is simple, writes one of the most articulate and expert of television producers committed to a fairly radical position on worship, Ian MacKenzie, the BBC's Head of Religious Programmes for Scotland:

> God is in the editing channel, in the studio, and in the room at home. The material being used – airwaves, machinery, electronic patter, film – these are, in God's hands, and in caring human hands, the bread and wine, broken, shared, for the world. That is liturgy.

Ian MacKenzie is too accomplished a theologian to fall into the gnostic pit he seems to skirt by a whisker in his views about television worship. None the less, if the conservative tends to be too pedantically materialist in his understanding of television worship, the radical threatens to spiritualise religious community to an extent which cannot be reconciled with any Christian understanding of incarnation.

There is one programme series, 'This is the Day', being developed by the BBC and transmitted to a highly appreciative audience, which is a fascinating fusion of conservative and radical elements in television worship.

'This is the Day' abandons totally the convention of the church setting. Worship comes from a home and is transmitted to viewers sitting in front of their television sets in identical circumstances to the family gathered under the camera's eye. They pray and read the Scriptures and hear a short sermon.

The imagery which illustrates these traditional activities is cast in the idiom of television to convey the sense that what is happening is a genuine *television* experience. The viewers are not spectators looking in on the doings of the family whose worship is being televised; an electronic open circuit has been set up which the viewer is invited to hook into. The television screen thus becomes an icon, an object upon which are graven pictures intended to stimulate devotion.

At the beginning of the programme, viewers at home are invited to light a candle and put it on the television set together with a hunk of bread. At the climax of the service, the preacher breaks bread and hands it to the members of the family from whose home the service is coming; the viewer is invited to break and eat bread at the same time. It is spelt out that the breaking of bread is in no way intended to be some form of televisual mass or eucharist; no words of consecration are spoken over it.

There are two technical reasons for the act of breaking bread. Others of the viewer's senses besides sight and sound can be engaged in touching, smelling and eating the bread, so it becomes more nearly a fully corporeal act. And it is an act in which simultaneous participation overleaps some of the inevitable isolation of the television experience. The production team thought of it theologically as a species of the old Primitive Methodist love feast or even that oldest of all gestures of human solidarity and fellowship, the symbolic meal. Professor J. G. Davies in a most welcome theological commentary on 'This is the Day' in the journal *Theology* suggests another interpretation.

Apparently, at the end of the Eucharist in the Eastern Orthodox churches, bread intended specifically for non-communicants and known as the 'antidoron' is blessed and distributed. It is for the benefit of those who cannot technically be in communion with one another and yet seek some symbol of Christian fellowship. Professor Davies goes

on to propose a pastoral ministry for television viewers
watching 'This is the Day' based on the notion of the reserved
sacrament:

> The local minister, knowing that a transmission is to take place
> and having compiled a list of those wishing to communicate but
> unable to be present at church, has only to take or arrange for the
> delivery beforehand of the reserved sacrament so that it may be
> consumed at the same time as the act of communion in the
> church building witnessed on the screen.

Professor Davies sees television services as catering for
three categories of viewers:

> For the 'faithful' the delivery of the reserved sacrament and for
> those requesting it the blessed bread. This last would be
> consumed either at the climax of 'This is the Day' or at the end of
> the Eucharist, exactly as the antidoron in the Eastern Orthodox
> churches. The third category of viewers comprises those who
> seek neither the eucharistised nor the blessed bread but would
> wish to continue to appreciate 'This is the Day' without any link
> additional to the existing symbolic gesture of fellowship...

Professor Davies's proposal is welcome for two reasons. It
might go some way to forging a link between television
worship and pastoral ministry. And the fact that a
distinguished theologian is giving attention to what goes on
in this area of religious broadcasting helps to ease the sense
of isolation felt by television worship producers who are
prone to feel they operate in a no-man's-land between the
Churches and the vast congregation of television-set owners.

A format such as 'This is the Day', once it has been refined,
may prove to be the nearest worship can get to being a
television event. Not for the first time in Christian history,
the holding in tension of radical and conservative positions
may provide a creative compromise.

While arguments continue between radicals and conservatives about TV worship, the great set-piece national
occasions, the major Christian festivals and the services
traditionally associated with them are exempted from

serious challenge. This is because they fall into the category of television spectacle. That may not be the intention of those who plan and take part in them, but it is what television does to events of a certain scale and style.

Television *authenticates* the spectacle as a traditional and valued feature of national life. The Trooping of the Colour, the Cenotaph Service, the Last Night of the Proms – viewers are reassured by such televised events that all is still well in the land, and they identify themselves enthusiastically with what is on the screen. This is television acting as tribal minstrel.

Otherwise, televised worship remains a sacred conundrum. Some drastic restatement of the theology of mission is required to unravel it. And this can only come from the Churches not the TV authorities. A few brave spirits only are prepared to embrace and commend the notion of a Church that exists solely in the ether, whose members' relationship to God might better be described as *private* rather than *personal*. Some words of G. K. Chesterton in his *Introduction to the Book of Job* are pertinent: 'A man can no more possess a private religion than he can possess a private sun and moon.'

SEVEN

More Pressure Points of Religious TV

The Question of Balance

As we have seen, in the days of Lord Reith the BBC was openly committed to communicating Christian values. In 1948, the then Director-General, Sir William Haley, addressing the British Council of Churches said:

> There are many demands of impartiality laid on the Corporation, but this [about Christian values] is not one of them. We are citizens of a Christian country and the BBC – an institution set up by the State – bases its policy upon a positive attitude towards the Christian values. It seeks to safeguard those values and to foster acceptance of them. The whole preponderant weight of its programmes is directed towards this end.[18]

Seventeen years later, the Director-General of the time, Sir Hugh Greene, also insisted that the BBC could not be neutral or impartial about some issues. Where, for instance,

> there are clashes for and against the basic moral values, truthfulness, justice, freedom, compassion, tolerance. Nor do I believe we should be impartial about certain things like racialism or extreme forms of political belief.

In that short period of less than a quarter of a century, the BBC's championship of Christian values had given place to a concern for moral values in general and for tolerance above all else. Under the earlier dispensations, religious broadcasting need not apologise for its more dogmatic affirmations – the department was reflecting the ethos of a Christian country. But from the 'seventies onwards, critics began to ask why religious broadcasting did not observe the concept of balance which was the BBC's policy about other controversial matters.

The commitment of the BBC and later the IBA to broadcast all opinions other than those subversive of freedom or which outrage public decency created a new situation for religious broadcasting in a post-Christian society. It crystallised into the question of the right of devotees of faiths other than Christianity or of no faith to have access to the airwaves.

The broadcasting authorities have frequently acknowledged their responsibility to reflect the religious beliefs and experience of British people who are adherents of great faiths such as Judaism, Islam, Hinduism and Sikhism. The problem is a technical one – how to do it in ways which are neither patronising nor misleading and still constitute true *broad*casting, given that the sacred language of the faith may not be English. The right of those who profess no religious faith, such as humanists, to a share in *religious* broadcasting is more contentious.

Some of the more conservative Church leaders take the view that religious television and radio only exist at all because a majority of the public feel it important to have one area of broadcasting which explores the person's relationship with God. Since humanists and their allies do not believe in any God, how could they logically expect to appear on programmes produced by the religious departments of the two authorities?

A parallel argument, advanced by Christians who have some sympathy with the humanist case for a voice on radio and television, is to the effect that the crusade against revealed religion is only one theme in contemporary humanism, and a minor one at that. Humanism in one form or another is probably the unacknowledged faith of the vast majority of broadcasters, so humanist ideas freely permeate the general output already.

It could be argued that the list of virtues catalogued by Sir

Hugh Greene in 1965 – tolerance, justice, truthfulness, compassion and freedom – *are* humanist values, all of which Christians interpret in a quite special sense. So the BBC has moved from a Reithian era, in which the purpose of *all* broadcasting was to further Christian values, to one in which general broadcasting's operating philosophy is humanist, with religious broadcasting having a specialist role in exploring the theistic interpretation of life.

Some of the tougher-minded humanist organisations accept the logic of the conservative Christian position that religious broadcasting should concern itself with God rather than No-God. So they are lobbying vigorously for the complete abolition of specialist religious departments in radio and television. They have a bizarre problem. In general, the only area of television which is prepared to give humanists an opportunity to discuss their religious ideas *is* the Religious Department.

The general programme departments of the television service, such as current affairs and documentaries, tend to regard the humanist and rationalist organisations, rightly or wrongly, as throw-backs from the nineteenth century. Many television producers regard both religious organisations and rationalist associations with equal scepticism. Humanist ideas may fascinate them and inform their behaviour but they see little value in 'churches'. So humanist preachers get short shrift from general television.

Arguments about balance or lack of it in religious television get most intense at the point where the programmes deal with matters which have political implications. Broadcasters in the current affairs and general programme areas have to ensure that spokesmen of both the Left and Right are given a platform when contentious political subjects are dealt with. They sometimes complain that religious television flouts this rule with impunity. It certainly seems so to Christians of a particular political persuasion when they claim to detect partisan bias against them in religious programmes.

No one who has wrestled with the issues thrown up at the points where the Gospel intersects and challenges the life of society needs to be directed towards the root of the problem. It lies primarily not in human fallibility and partiality but in the nature of the Gospel itself. A summary statement of the case might run as follows.

Christianity is a historical religion. All its key events have happened in recorded time and not in the realms of mythology. Hence the work of salvation is not confined to private transactions between the individual soul and God; it is advanced or held back by what happens in the life of this and every nation because the Gospel speaks to men and women in their togetherness. According to the New Testament, the goal of Christian discipleship is the transformation of the present world order into a new creation along the lines of a blueprint spelt out in the life and teaching of Jesus.

If this is so, then Christian commentary on contemporary events is not the prerogative of trendy clergymen or long-haired Lefties – to quote the stereotypes – but is a central thrust of the Judaeo-Christian tradition. It is unthinkable that a religious broadcasting department committed to exploring *every* aspect of faith in its programmes should slide away from this one because it might be contentious.

Christianity is also an incarnate faith which means that the Christian is called to seek out, identify and draw attention to the places and events in which he or she believes Christ to be at work throughout the world. And if the Gospels are anything to go by, Jesus is to be sought in some very murky and controversial places. The cameras and microphones must go where the broadcasters perceive Christ. So the themes of religious programmes will often explore politically and ethically sensitive areas of society, with public outcry sometimes the result.

Religious broadcasters apply a rough rule of thumb to the business of balance. It isn't foolproof and sometimes breaks down, but they try to distinguish between Christian *principles* and the *policy* options which flow from those principles. 'Principle' is probably too rigid and precise a term for what is better understood as some Christian consensus about the content of the Gospel.

Broadcasters do not believe they have any obligation to balance statements of Christian principle in their programmes because the BBC and IBA both determined at the outset that equal time should not be given to God and the Devil. But because there can be an enormous gulf between any Christian principle and its practical application, policy options ought to be balanced where possible.

There are those who argue that this distinction between Christian principles and policies is illusory. Since it is 'by his fruits' that the Christian is known, there are no Christian principles, *only* policies – Christianity is a way and not a law or even a philosophy. The religious broadcaster, however, has to have some practical way of determining what can be stated without challenge and what ought to be balanced; hence, this rough and ready working distinction between principle and policy.

There are, of course, some things about which Jesus said absolutely nothing. His alleged attitude towards a whole plethora of contemporary issues can only be derived by analogy from the Gospels, by dissecting Biblical texts or through sheer inspired guesswork. The gnomic and sometimes perverse sayings of Jesus first spoken in a rural backwater of the Roman Empire two thousand years ago do not yield too many imperatives capable of easy application in a complex modern world.

The problem is complicated by the fact that the very Christian principles which religious producers believe are exempt from the requirement of balance are actually *biased* according to any notion of natural justice the average viewer is likely to hold. The Gospel is not even-handed and objective in its treatment of all sorts and conditions of people. Jesus displays not simply fair-mindedness but downright favouritism towards the outcast, underprivileged and disadvantaged. When religious television follows suit, those sections of society which do not fall into these categories scream outrage.

Jesus seems also to have been sceptical of all concentrations of earthly power. He distanced himself from Establishments, however defined – ecclesiastical, political or cultural. There is, therefore, a radical, authority-questioning tinge to even the most faithful paraphrase of Christian principles. It cannot be 'balanced' out of existence without doing violence to the Gospel record.

Many viewers who detect this radical undertone to religious programmes are quick to label it 'left-wing'. This is usually a mistaken opinion. If the word 'radical' has any directional reference, it is downward towards the root of a matter rather than to Left or Right.

Religious producers are allowed a degree of freedom not enjoyed anywhere else throughout broadcasting. Allied to this freedom is access to the levers of immense media-power. In the end they will always be held accountable for what they do, but in the short run they have the capacity for great mischief unless power is combined with reticence.

Nothing devalues Christian prophecy more than the tendency to be garrulous about matters of great moment in the contemporary world. Television producers are not immune from this temptation. They have their favourite 'issues' to which they return again and again until, regrettably, the viewer reacts to a matter of some importance with a very big yawn.

It is an axiom of all forms of prophetic utterance, not excluding television, that the benefit of the doubt should always be given to those bearing grievous national burdens. Politicians, industrialists, trades-union moguls, financiers, princes of the Church or of the realm are easy targets. They live and sometimes perish in the white light of the public arena. Majestic imprecations from positions of non-responsibility are alien to the spirit of Christ. They also indicate the bankruptcy of the communicator's professional integrity.

In religious television of the studio discussion variety, it is not too difficult for most viewers to size up an argument and decide whether they are being given a true bill of goods – the pure seed of the faith rather than a lot of contentious chaff. But what about the television documentary where opinion is built into the structure of the film without being clearly labelled? That question is only part of a much more fundamental debate about the 'religiousness' of religious television.

How Religious is Religious TV?

'Much too religious!' insists the general viewer looking in on a televised worship service and commenting sourly that he is staying away from his local church in order not to have to endure what he is being presented with on the screen.

'Not half religious enough!' comment some traditional believers, watching a religious documentary about a subject so alien to their experience that they cannot credit its provenance as the Religious Department of the BBC or ITV. They understand a religious subject to be one in which the Church is given high visibility. They may go even further and claim that it is the job of religious broadcasting to be an arm of the Church's outreach.

A deceptively simple view is that religious television is concerned with religious subjects in the same way that 'Panorama' deals with politics, 'Horizon' with science and 'Omnibus' with music and the arts. But this only pushes the problem one stage further back. What *is* a religious subject?

According to Penry Jones, former Head of Religious Broadcasting at the BBC, 'All television is religious television' – which offers the programme-maker an unconditional licence to poke around in the plenitude of life and come up with themes that fascinate him. Evangelicals, on the other hand, claim that all religious television should directly or indirectly testify to the Lordship of Christ.

A common-sense approach to the problem might be to decide that the subject matter of religious programmes is irrelevant, it is the viewer who makes the final judgment about whether a programme is or is not 'really' religious. If the penny drops and he experiences such things as wonder, awe, a sense of otherness, inspiration, contrition, deep peace, or if he undergoes a radical change of mind or heart then the programme qualifies as genuinely religious.

Historically, certain subjects and themes have proved efficacious in evoking religious emotions or offering spiritual insights. But subject matter is an unreliable test of religious authenticity. Both militant atheism and passionate theism could well produce an identical agenda of subjects and themes.

If the viewer's needs define religious television rather than programme subjects, it follows that the religious departments of television have no monopoly of religious programmes. Nor should they have. Yet it is a little haphazard to put the viewer's religious experience at the mercy of his or her knob-twiddling capacity. A TV religious department must surely tackle the problem in a more systematic way or forfeit the right to a separate existence.

The test-case is the religious documentary, for unlike a televised event such as the church service, it has been created exclusively for the medium.

Some evangelical Christians argue that there is no problem. Get devout believers to make a committed documentary on a subject of central Christian importance, let them pray over it as well as work at it and the result must be undeniably a truly religious product. The sad truth is that it is likely to appeal only to those for whom television is a mirror for reflecting the faith they already hold.

How, then, is it possible, without being propagandist, to create documentaries which significant numbers of viewers perceive to be authentically religious for them? A most valuable notion uses an industrial analogy – the documentary subject as raw material with religious 'value' added at each stage in the production process. The final result is successful to the extent that this accretion of religious value is perceived by a viewer.

I offer an example in which I was personally involved – a documentary in the 'Everyman' series about changes in the Church's missionary strategy. It was called 'A Long Way from Home'.

The first level of religious interpretation was that of the series producer of 'Everyman' when confronted with a proposal that the film should be made. Leaving aside technical questions about cost, availability of resources and accessibility of locations, he pondered whether a film based on the proposed idea would fit into his series. Did it accord with his understanding of the aims of 'Everyman'? Was it a genuinely religious subject *and* one which lent itself to documentary treatment?

An editor's own religious sensitivities, his background, experience and reading will be brought to bear on any idea to test its suitability for a religious series. Then he must decide whether it will make a good story. Could a strong narrative thread join a significant question to either a firm conclusion or the laying bare of a dilemma? And is the question one that will interest viewers anyway?

The second level of interpretation was that added to the basic idea by me as the one through whose eyes the viewer would follow the story. What point was I trying to make about modern missionary strategy? In which locations would the supporting evidence be found? How could dissenting views be incorporated into the documentary so that the viewer could make up his mind about the soundness of my idea?

My theme, in brief, was that the old style of Christian mission, which was entirely one-way – from the 'Christian' West to the 'heathen' lands beyond the seas, was giving place to a strategy of mission that had Christians on the move in all directions, and, surprisingly, *to* the West *from* Africa and Asia.

The embryonic structure which emerged at this stage took the form of a journey which I, as an ex-African missionary, would take back to Africa to find out what changes in the strategy of mission had occurred in the twenty-five years since I first set foot in the dark continent.

My journey from location to location would provide the thread of the film with interviews in each place supplying the supporting evidence. The film therefore was to begin with my arrival at Nairobi airport and end with the arrival at Heathrow of an African missionary to Britain with his family.

A highly complicated issue would have to be simplified to a degree which some experts in the field might claim was unacceptable distortion. Besides being oversimplified the story was also likely to be overdramatised because the viewer demands action – a documentary without pace withers on the vine.

By far the most important level of interpretation was that provided by the film's producer/director. He had to make all the key on-the-spot decisions about what to film and in what tone of voice – strongly affirmative or low-key. Equally crucially, he must decide what could not be filmed because it would take too much time or push the film over its budget through transport or film costs. Hence, a witness might say, 'Colin Morris is talking bosh about missionary work! I can show you a mission station a hundred miles from here where this and that and the other is going on which proves him wrong.'

Such a comment would place the producer in a dilemma. He wants to get at the truth, and yet the making of a documentary is not a 'time and money no object' exercise. He is working to a carefully planned schedule, especially in Africa where distances are vast and transport services both scarce and very expensive. To move a seven man and woman team an additional hundred miles could add thousands of pounds to the cost of the film and throw out by a couple of days carefully arranged rendezvous in other places.

The producer has to make such critical decisions a dozen times a day while on location. And he must do so with a nagging question always lurking in the back of his mind, 'Is there really a story here that we can actually get on to the screen, or shall we return to Britain with thousands of feet of beautiful film but no honest documentary?'

At all costs the producer must resist the temptation of trying to 'invent' a story which isn't there. The finished film will be pointless and the viewer is sure to sense the fact.

Every creative professional lives with the temptation of making his work self-justifying. Peter Armstrong, one of the most accomplished of religious documentary producers, puts it this way:

> In choosing which story line to take there is always the temptation to choose one which makes the best television rather than one which is religiously the most illuminating. One

interpretation might make the programme more entertaining, another might allow scope for beautiful photography, a third might be chosen because it enhances the producer's professional reputation as an investigative journalist . . . This is the real point of threat to the religious integrity of a documentary.

Through all the decisions he made, the producer had to give the finished film its official tone of voice. It was his duty to guarantee to the viewer the contents of the film as an honest account of the truth as he saw it. In this role he was 'Mr BBC', putting on the line the Corporation's reputation for integrity and high standards of truthfulness, to assure viewers that they were not being deceived nor subjected to propaganda disguised as objective reporting.

The fourth level of interpretation of the missionary film was added during the process of editing the thousands of feet of film and marrying sound to pictures. The uncut film had to be viewed again and again and slowly reduced to its final length. As a general rule, ten times as much film is shot as is actually used, so for every foot of film which appeared in the transmitted version, nine feet would end up lying on the cutting-room floor.

Of that mountain of discarded footage, much of it was the consequence of having to shoot scenes again and again to get them right. But some were sequences of perfectly acceptable technical quality which had to be discarded because they would extend the argument of the film beyond its decreed length or introduce a digression. It is over rejected sequences that the most furious arguments always rage in the cutting room.

In the later stages of cutting 'A Long Way from Home', the editor of the 'Everyman' series, reviewing the material, had to confirm or modify the producer's stance, varying the length of sequences or insisting on others being added. In the end, he had to decide whether in the miles of film there was a story at all that he wanted to transmit as part of his series. If not, then in spite of the huge financial cost and the dedicated skill that had gone into the project, he would refuse to allow it to be seen by the viewer. It had not matched up to his standards of technical excellence, of journalistic integrity and religious insight.

Viewers, of course, were the final judges of the religious value of the documentary. What did they make of the film? Firstly, as entertainment. If they lost interest and switched off their sets all the agonising about religious value was wasted effort. The film had failed in its primary purpose, which was not to recruit viewers to the cause of Christian world mission – that is the job of the Churches – but to occupy their mind agreeably for a given period of television time.

Assuming the film passed the first test and was sufficiently gripping to hold some viewers' attention as television entertainment, what they made of the documentary then depended very much on their own personal convictions. If they were traditionally religious they might have reacted unsympathetically to any novel approach to Christian mission which did not reinforce what they already believed. They could, therefore, conclude that the programme was not genuinely religious, but an attempt to undermine true Christianity.

At the other end of the scale, the agnostic viewers' reactions were probably vaguer. They would not be disposed to judge religious documentaries by different standards from those which apply throughout the rest of the television output. Using the yardstick of current-affairs series such as 'Panorama' or 'World in Action', they would decide whether or not the programme was a 'good' one according to the honesty of its reporting.

Religious documentaries must always negotiate this veracity tight-rope. If they are not as objective as current-affairs programmes such as 'Panorama' they will not convince the general viewer about their truthfulness. But if in meeting this requirement they are indistinguishable from the general run of current-affairs documentaries, they will sell the dummy on religion and throw back at the viewer his or her own agnostic attitudes towards the world.

Possibly, the best we could hope for is that viewers, in reflecting on what they had seen, might become sensitised to religious questions which had never occurred to them before.

What happens next would be more problematical. The television caravan moves on. In the evening-long stream of programmes, a documentary sinks in the memory and the viewer's attention is attracted to the next package of wares on offer in the electronic market-place. But if the documentary has done its job, the questions raised by it have become part of public discourse to which the Churches and other bodies with a special interest can respond.

This is one of the key questions of Christian communication in the television age. How can the religious output of a public service broadcasting organisation and the response of the Churches be synchronised without a privileged relationship being set up which the BBC's Charter or the IBA's Act of Parliament would outlaw?

Christian television stations of the American type have no such problems. Their programmes are honestly propagandist and they can follow a common strategy with the religious organisations or denominations that finance them. But public service broadcasting is debarred from engaging in propaganda even of such a high-minded kind.

The dilemma is obvious. Unlike the Churches, religious television has no mandate to recruit viewers to a lifetime vocation in the service of the truth it conveys. Unlike television, the Churches can no longer get their version of the truth in living colour into virtually every home. Thus far, we are miles away from any workable solution to this problem of complementarity between religious media and religious constituencies.

The Television Sabbath
When BBC Television began to transmit regular programmes, the shape of the media Sunday was modelled on the early days of radio. There were no television programmes at all on Sundays until after 7.30 pm. The rationale was twofold. Television ought not to be ensnaring potential worshippers away from church services; and Sunday's traditional role as a day of rest should also encompass a ·

respite from electronically transmitted entertainment.

Public pressure for a comprehensive television service on Sundays soon became irresistible. This demand was reinforced by the results of population surveys and the doleful observation of the Churches themselves that, with a number of regional and denominational variations, the Sunday evening worship service seemed to be in irreversible decline. And this before television offered any serious competition.

In 1955, the Postmaster-General, who regulated the number of hours every week that BBC Television could transmit, ruled that Sunday should become a standard weekend television day. Out of deference to the Churches, he insisted that there should be a 'closed period' between 6.15 p.m. and 7.30 p.m. when no television programmes were to be transmitted. The traditional church worship hour at least would not resound to the noise of electronic Babel.

When ITV came on the scene, adventurously, they got permission to transmit religious programmes in the closed period. The BBC did the same shortly afterwards. The Central Religious Advisory Committee (CRAC) which from the early days had advised the BBC, was also given the responsibility of keeping an eye on ITV and began to monitor these programmes.

CRAC gloomily concluded that it was probably too late to prevent the drift away from Sunday evening church-going. Television might have steepened the decline, but the causes of this defection lay deep in British social history. So the closed period on television should be used creatively as a shady spot where religious programmes could be nurtured, sheltered from the howling gales of competition offered by general television entertainment.

A formal closed period on both BBC and ITV on Sundays between 6.15 p.m. and 7.25 p.m. became the test-bed for many kinds of innovation and experiment. Newly fledged religious producers had a fairly tension-free apprenticeship, not having to fear the heavy competition which makes for caution and reliance on well-tried programme formats. But as these producers gained in confidence and experience, the closed period began increasingly to irk them. They were tired of the nursery slope; they wished to launch themselves down the mountain and take their chances against all opposition.

In 1976, the BBC therefore proposed to ITV and to CRAC that the closed period should be halved in the early evening to run from 6.40 p.m. to 7.15 p.m. and that another 35 minutes of religious programmes should be transmitted later in the evening, around 10.15 p.m.

ITV preferred to retain the old closed period for their own religious programmes, but gave their blessing to the BBC's proposal. So religion, in the first instance a documentary series, 'Everyman', would attempt the perilous task of holding its own against the heavy competition of popular late Sunday evening programmes on BBC-2 and ITV.

Inevitably, given the responsibilities of public service broadcasting, certain other types of programme had over the years been admitted into the closed period – programmes for the deaf, or in the Welsh language. More balefully, since television thrives by getting the hotly topical into viewers' homes at the first possible moment, it was argued that certain live events which were taking place during the closed period would be lost unless they could be transmitted there and then. This became the crack in the dam wall through which torrents of live sport were later to pour.

When BBC-2 was established, it was argued that there should be no unfair competition in programming against the closed period on BBC-1 and ITV. The types of programme which should be permitted were not detailed but left to the good sense and discrimination of the Controller of BBC-2. And with the advent of a second ITV channel, Channel Four, the gentleman's agreement to do the decent thing by religious programmes was accepted by the Controller of the new channel.

Major powers of prophecy are not needed to see the end of these present arrangements. Religious television has come of age. Religious programmes are being scheduled for days other than Sunday. It is too early to assess how mid-week religious programmes will fare against heavy competition *and* the challenge of appearing on a day when viewers have not traditionally expected them to be shown. Satellite and cable will also multiply the number of TV channels and it is unthinkable that there should be a closed period on *all* of them.

The broadcasters' responsibility to reflect the concerns of great faiths other than Christianity also puts a question-mark against the closed period. Sunday is not the Holy Day of Jews or Muslims, for example, so they are not seized of the importance of the link between religious programmes and the Christian Sabbath. Nor has even the most liberal-minded of them any burning desire to see programmes about Christianity specially protected.

The changing shape of Sunday on television has been most influenced by the pressures of 'mature' secularity operating throughout society. Major sporting events such as test-matches are now played on Sundays, there is growing clamour to amend outmoded sabbatarian laws and the Churches have lost the power to determine the nature of the day. Forty years of national ambiguity about the religious significance of Sunday is now hardening into unashamed non-observance.

For the vast majority of television viewers, Sunday is simply the second half and climax of the weekend and they expect programmes with mass appeal. Religious programmes though usually regarded by channel controllers as having only minority interest were given highly desirable time-placings in the old, relaxed days. Now that Sunday evening is the key battleground of the week where the BBC and ITV clash for a lion's share of the viewing public, religious programmes will be under constant threat because they are thought, rightly or wrongly, to be 'audience-losers'.

When religious broadcasters, uncertain what policies they ought to fight for, turn to the Churches for guidance about the modern Sunday, they encounter disarray. Some sections of the Churches are unremittingly Sabbatarian in their attitudes and would ban Sunday television altogether if they could. The rest seem agreed only in bewailing the fact that television itself has accelerated the decline into godlessness.

Then they advocate varying degrees of compromise with the inevitable.

Edwin Robertson, the veteran religious broadcaster, is one of the few modern theologians who has given any attention to the nature of the contemporary Sunday and the media's role in it. He takes as his starting-point the Bible's insistence on the two-pronged observance of the Sabbath – the Deuteronomic instruction – 'You shall remember that you were a servant in the land of Egypt, therefore the Lord commanded you to keep the Sabbath' – coupled with Jesus' words, 'Do good and not evil on the Sabbath, save life and not destroy it.'

Holiness and compassion are, therefore, the two elements in true Sabbath observance. Sunday is the appropriate day to blend religious and humanitarian activities.

Though church-going is now a minority activity on Sunday, a much wider sector of society approves of it, argues Robertson. There is an almost superstitious belief that society as a whole benefits if churches are open and the devout busy themselves praying for the rest. Churches are expected to hold religious services, and radio and television channels are expected to transmit religious programmes. They are all symbols of the divine in national life, and valued in a vague sort of way by that majority of non church-goers who tell the pollsters they still believe in God.

The cult of the family which is centred on Sunday is also of pseudo-religious significance. Saturday means sport, organised entertainment and parties. Sunday is for domestic activities such as cleaning the car, gardening, visiting relatives and afternoon naps. While Robertson concedes that the clean distinction between Saturday and Sunday has become blurred, he insists it can still be discerned.

The public's expectation, however shadowy, that Sunday should be different, is reflected on television, Robertson says. Programmes take account of the family nature of the day by being less explicit. Humour is moderated, satire is less savage and feature films are usually not of the hard-nosed variety.

Viewers demand this subtle distinction between the two

days of the weekend not necessarily because they are very religious but because they have an innate sense of what is appropriate on the Sabbath which they no longer actively centre on the Church. It is a gut reaction rather than a reasoned response which has them protesting, 'It doesn't seem right!' when broadcasters overstep the mark.

Robertson invokes the sociologist F.A. Hayek, who claims that 'culture is neither natural nor artificial, neither genetically transmitted nor rationally designed. It is a tradition of learnt rules of conduct which have never been "invented" and whose functions the acting individuals usually do not understand.' This is how a ghostly Sunday observance is transmitted from generation to generation. The rules have not so much been handed on as absorbed through the skin and are not usually given formal shape or even consciously invoked.

The social element in Sunday observance, which embraces the concerns of compassion, Robertson believes is perpetuated in the popularity of marches and demonstrations about political and ethical issues. These gatherings show that a section of society has a strong urge to assert social justice. The rest of society has never pronounced that Sunday is an inappropriate day for demonstrations, however much it may disapprove of the convictions of some marchers.

Television's response to the social dimension of Sunday is twofold. The Sunday TV news-bulletins usually carry reasonably full coverage of demonstrations and marches. Indeed, the timing and location of these events is usually planned so as to make things easy for television crews. And religious television makes a response to the humanitarian emphasis of Sunday by transmitting documentary series such as the BBC's 'Everyman' or ITV's 'Credo' which deal robustly with issues at the interface between faith and society.

Religious broadcasters are greatly reassured by Edwin Robertson's insistence, supported by CRAC, that such documentaries are not, as some conservative Christians claim, desecrating the Sabbath with social concerns. They are a legitimate visual response to the claim of Jesus that the

Sabbath is supremely the day on which to advance the claims of compassion and highlight the needs and rights of our neighbour.

I would go further and argue that these television explorations of political and social issues are consonant with the command to maintain the holiness of Sunday. As every apprentice-preacher knows, 'holiness' is synonymous with 'wholeness'. The wholeness of faith represented on television requires a counterpoint between worship and documentary, programmes both of affirmation and of challenge. It is the *range* of religious programmes as well as their content which links the media Sabbath to its origins in the Bible.

If Hayek's 'learnt rules' imperceptibly affect the attitudes of viewers to Sunday, these rules are in turn being influenced by television. Television is both a reflector and an initiator. Society learns new values from television even as the medium is busy reflecting the values which already exist.

The conclusion must be, therefore, that television is evolving its own Sabbath, marked off from Saturday in ways that echo both the Christian origins of Sunday and the social attitudes and values which have filled the vacuum left by its decline. Most religious programmes will continue to be scheduled on Sundays because public service broadcasting authorities show a keen sense of history and tradition.

The BBC and IBA have a concern for the 'wholeness' of life which is a secular expression of the Christian imperative to holiness. They want all areas of creative endeavour to be represented on the small screen, and especially those which have helped to mould the essential genius of the British people.

As students of the psychology of television, the broadcasting authorities are aware that the viewer is receptive to some subjects and themes at certain times and on certain days. Beyond that, it is up to the religious broadcasters to see that the content and range of their programmes testify to the twofold Biblical concern for the holiness and compassion of Sunday.

Of course, once television cable systems are well-established and home video-recorders become much cheaper and wider-spread throughout society, the viewer will determine for himself the shape of his television Sabbath. Then will be starkly revealed all kinds of things about the fundamental religious nature of our society which those responsible for religious broadcasting only purport to see in a glass darkly at present.

An Afterword on Defining Religious Broadcasting

In the late 'fifties, the BBC told the Pilkington Committee that the objectives of religious broadcasting were to reflect the worship, thought and action of those Churches which represent the mainstream of the Christian tradition in Britain, to stress what is most relevant in the Christian faith for the modern world and to try to reach those outside the Churches. In 1977, CRAC told the Annan Committee that the old Pilkington guidelines were in need of revision and reinterpretation. CRAC proposed instead these three propositions as the objective of religious broadcasting:

1. To seek to reflect the worship, thought and action of the principal religious traditions represented in Britain, recognising that these traditions are mainly though not exclusively Christian;
2. To seek to present to viewers and listeners those beliefs, ideas, issues and experiences in the contemporary world which are evidently related to a religious interpretation or dimension of life;
3. To seek also to meet the religious interests, concerns and needs of those on the fringe of, or outside, the organised life of the Churches.

In under two decades, CRAC had moved from a traditionally Christian definition of the aims of religious broadcasting to one which took account of the fact Christianity and religion were no longer synonymous in Britain. In the years since Annan reported, the climate of religious opinion has become even more opaque.

The objectives of religious broadcasting submitted to and

accepted by the Annan Committee remain a valuable
working guide to what broadcasters in the field are about.
Certainly, the phrases are widely quoted in the vigorous
public debate which goes on ceaselessly about religious
broadcasting. But CRAC's threefold scheme is actually a
description rather than a definition. It sets out what a
religious broadcasting department should be doing rather
than what it is for – possibly wisely, to avoid imposing a
simplistic definition on a complex reality.

Nevertheless, because boundary disputes abound in
broadcasting organisations when departments compete for
scarce cash and resources, definition is a matter of more than
academic significance. It becomes a highly political issue.
For like all large institutions, broadcasting corporations are
for ever rationalising and reorganising their structures.
Hence, any department which does not have a clearly
marked out area of output which differentiates it from others
will be under threat whenever the latest managerial Lego
specialist starts taking things apart and putting them
together again.

Because life does not obligingly allow itself to be divided
up into a finite number of discrete elements to the reportage
of which a different operational team can be assigned, some
overlap in broadcasting output is inevitable. For instance,
all serious programme departments have a concern for what
might loosely be called the human condition, so they will
legitimately stray into each other's territory. The election of
an Archbishop of Canterbury might equally preoccupy both
news and religious departments. A human-rights story is as
much the business of the religious department as documentary features, current affairs or education. At this level,
the division of a broadcasting organisation into discrete
departments is as much a matter of historical circumstance
and administrative convenience as the demands of subject
areas.

In the end, however, a religious department must be able
to mark out ground which it is uniquely qualified to plough
if it is to survive. It is not, of course, by any means a
universally applauded notion that religious departments

ought to survive. Understandably, the British Humanist Association would like to see religious broadcasting departments abolished; more surprisingly, the Annan Committee recommended that they should be disbanded and the skills and experience thus freed applied throughout the rest of the service. 'There is no reason why religion should not be present as an influence in all programmes, reminding the moralists of spiritual values and the social scientists of the inevitability of individual moral choice.'

It is significant that the Annan Committee in describing the contribution religious broadcasters, if dispersed, could make to other areas of output chose to characterise religion in terms of spiritual values and moral choice. The factor which seems to me normative of religious broadcasting – worship – was left by Annan suspended in mid-air. They confessed that coping with worship would be a problem if religious departments were disbanded, and left it at that.

But if a definition of religious broadcasting were to be attempted, it is surely in the area represented, however problematically, by broadcast worship that the key is to be found. A religious broadcasting department justifies its separate existence in the last resort because its subject matter is religious faith – what it is, what it does and what its consequences are.

Religious broadcasting is about religious faith – which is not as tautological as it sounds. There are two assumptions implicit in the use of the term 'religious faith' as the key signature of religious broadcasting. One is that this faith has its source in some transcendent power. The second is that it embraces not just Christianity but *any* expression of faith which acknowledges the transcendent.

In practice, a religious department deals with religious faith in three ways according to a division which is crude and imprecise but serviceable: *what it is* – programmes of exposition, teaching and argument; *how it is awakened, celebrated and sustained* – programmes of worship, meditation and reflection; and *what its personal and social consequences are* – documentaries, testimonies and drama.

Now, if religious faith is defined as the human response to

the transcendent, it follows, somewhat surprisingly given the technical and theological difficulties, that the linchpin of a religious broadcasting department's output must be worship. For worship is about people addressing the transcendent directly. In doing so, they testify to the fact that the rationale of the religious department is not illusory. Other areas of output may be more topical, popular or generally significant, but they are derivative because they take as read the issue which worship tackles head-on.

The contentious question, is this a genuine religious programme? thus resolves itself into two others. What is religious faith doing in the contemporary world? And the answers might range from celebrating to suffering by way of all the dilemmas, emotions and reactions faith evokes. The second question is its complement. What does the contemporary world look like through the eyes of faith? Might we be able to see through to the truth behind the facts of an issue because of our distinctive perspective?

When we deal with matters of religious faith in the world, the subject usually reveals and justifies the programme's provenance. When we try to look at the world through the eyes of faith, the approach is the thing; the subject is likely to be utterly secular. Here is located the mine-field we do not always manage to negotiate without suffering shrapnel wounds.

In this area, the department is caught between one strand of opinion which believes religion should observe a godly silence about all worldly matters, and another that insists religion ought to have something to say about everything under the sun. In fact, there are many issues where the religious thing to say is the sane, humane, truthful, honest thing. There is no magical ingredient in the mixture which is some arcane religious additive. The secular and religious perspectives are at one.

This is where strong nerves are needed. The temptation is to import into such an issue a number of religious categories which do not properly belong there in order to demonstrate that it was a genuinely religious subject all along. Then we are justifiably open to the charge that we have used religion gratuitously to validate a subject we have chosen for different reasons. If we resist this urge, as I am sure we must, we have to bear with fortitude the strictures of those who claim to detect nothing 'religious' in the programme.

Our best defence is the self-evident quality of the programme, the producer's hard-won reputation for integrity and the department's track record of usually knowing what it is doing.

Even then we sometimes get it badly wrong. In mitigation, it might be claimed that religion deals with a very subjective and ultimately intangible area of experience. Broadcasting copes best with areas capable of neat definition and having sharp boundaries. There is something about the untidiness of religion that wars with broadcasting's almost prissy sense of order. Most of religion's most significant events happen in secret and broadcasting, by definition, is in the business of abolishing secrets.

It is all a little like exploring darkest Africa. The bush is so dense we sometimes do not know we have crossed a frontier until someone starts shooting at us. That is no excuse, of course. We do not have to explore darkest Africa. We can stay at home in Clapham and catch the omnibus with a sense of near certainty, given the vagaries of London Transport, about our destination. But religious faith is not spread by rumination.

One further point about religious programmes that stir up public controversy. It is sometimes claimed both within the Churches and the BBC that if the Religious Department would only stick to making programmes of worship and the like we could avoid needless furore. Dare one whisper 'Falklands Thanksgiving Service'? That was a pukka service of worship if ever there was one – St Paul's Cathedral, Archbishop in the pulpit, Cardinal in the choir, Moderator of the Kirk in attendance. Yet almost every element in the service offended someone – the lessons chosen, the hymns not chosen, the prayers, the Archbishop's sermon . . .

The truth is that the Judaeo-Christian tradition has a paradoxical effect within society. On the one hand it conserves certain values and yet at the same time unleashes forces which challenge and may replace those values. And this conservative-radical tension is as likely to be found within the most traditional broadcast liturgy as in an outspoken documentary. If broadcast worship challenges no one, it is not because this type of religious activity is anodyne but because it is not good worship or not good communication.

EIGHT

Ideas in a World of Images

B. H. Streeter, the New Testament scholar, once calculated that apart from the forty days and forty nights in the wilderness about which we know virtually nothing, everything reported to have been said and done by Jesus in all four Gospels would have occupied only three weeks. Less than a month out of, shall we say, a thirty-year life? The rest is silence. And yet on that tiny scrap of narrative has been erected a vast pyramid of formal Christian knowledge, not only volumes but whole libraries of theology.

So although the heart of Christianity is a story about Jesus, the vast bulk of Christian knowledge, traditional theology, takes the form of abstract ideas – propositional statements about God, humanity and the world woven together in complex chains of logic. Great cataracts of words, arguments powerful and sometimes beautifully stated, counter-arguments refuted – miles and miles of print virtually bereft of any image accessible to the television camera lens.

Because television is an electronic story-teller, it can cope with the basic Christian narrative. But what does a visual medium do with a superstructure of abstract ideas that cannot be turned into pictures? Is it possible to do theology at all on television and if not, does it matter? Some theologians retort that theology is as much entitled to its technical language and special disciplines as, say, nuclear physics, and if television can't cope with it, then that's too bad.

The problem of visualising ideas, however, remains. And it is not the theologian's alone, but is shared with

philosophers, economic theorists and some species of pure
scientists.

Between 1973 and 1976 the BBC spent a vast sum of money
on a prestigious documentary series about the history of
economic ideas. They chose as presenter one of the wittiest
and most articulate of experts, Professor John Galbraith.
Eventually transmitted under the title 'The Age of Uncertainty' the series was generally judged by professionals to
have been an honourable failure.

Professor Galbraith and the producer were felt to have
acquitted themselves well. The depressing verdict was that
the medium had failed the message. The ideas were too
abstruse to be visualised convincingly even though the
filmed sequences were lavishly realised. What goes for
economic theory cannot augur well for abstract religious
ideas either.

The problem has two elements. There is the longstanding
antipathy and deep suspicion many intellectuals have for
television. And there is the innate resistance of the medium
itself to ideas.

The Revolt of the Intellectuals

In spite of infrequent experiments like the Galbraith series
the intellectual community and television producers have
traditionally observed a pact of mutual non-aggression.
They have kept well out of each other's way, though many
intellectuals (and this does not exclude theologians) have
made no secret of their disdain or even contempt for the
medium.

The classical intellectual view about television is that it is
a medium of mindless entertainment, a great trash-
generating engine which works against serious thought,
critical standards and profound values. In the early days of
television, it was considered a mark of intellectual virtue
never to have watched the small screen, then later on, never
to have owned a set, and still later, only to keep one in the
playroom for the children.

Recently, it has become fashionable for intellectuals to
declare an irrational weakness for the odd cult programme

such as 'Monty Python's Flying Circus' or 'Fawlty Towers'. 'I like my entertainment moronic,' confessed a Nobel Prize winner recently on radio, then pleaded guilty to getting hooked on 'Dallas'. He spoke in the regretful tones of someone owning up to a penchant for wife-beating.

The temperament of most intellectuals puts them at odds with the medium. Television is about *broad*casting. By definition it aims to reach and please a vast public. To do this, producers must strike at a popular level of programming, somewhere around mid-centre of public taste.

The intellectual aims his product in the first instance at an élite, his fellow intellectuals. It is a rare publicist who cares overmuch whether or not his ideas gain popular acceptance. So long as his peers approve, that is what chiefly matters.

It is also human nature to resent the work of those who vulgarise subjects we know a lot about. Television producers are lay people, they dabble for a few weeks in areas and fields to which some scholars have devoted their lives. Not only does television reduce a complex issue to a 25-minute oversimplified treatment, it compounds the offence in the eyes of the intellectual by handling it with such spurious authority and glamour that the viewer accepts without question the small screen's version as orthodoxy.

The intellectual community has not been without its prophets who have seized on the fact that television is an immensely powerful means of putting across information – instantaneous in its impact, clawing in its reach and clamant in its emotional appeal. So they embraced eagerly the harlot-medium from which their fellows used to recoil. Accepting the constraint of television, learning its disciplines, and venturing into the strange cosmos from which it operates, they have become master expositors. And celebrities.

The late and much lamented Professor Robert MacKenzie became the resident guru of current-affairs programmes, deploying knowledge in a simple, vivid style. He pranced around the small screen with an almost manic glee, interpreting political events and interviewing political personalities. The swingometer, his own invention to make the reading of election results simple, was a symbol of his willingness to abandon academic diffidence for highly visible, even brash exposition.

Before MacKenzie exploded on to the scene, the odd academic had somewhat sniffily agreed to appear in the 'heavier' political programmes on BBC-2, and to pontificate. MacKenzie and his producers took the gamble that he could hold the interest of the vast audiences who watched the more popular current-affairs programmes such as 'Nationwide' on BBC-1.

MacKenzie won a huge following of viewers, but at the price of sacrificing his academic purity. Some of his colleagues in the university world were less than amused by his antics. They made it plain to him that he had forfeited all right to be thought of as a serious scholar.

Dr David Butler of Nuffield College, Oxford, has also been willing to breach the academic *cordon sanitaire* around the BBC Television Centre. He introduced the viewing public to the curious science of psephology, the study of electoral behaviour. He has become an essential part of every major election telecast.

Less extroverted than MacKenzie, Butler's great feat has been to import some of the excitement of football-pool prediction into the solemn business of Government-choosing. Possibly because he operates in a more specialised field than Bob MacKenzie, David Butler has been judged an academic consultant rather than performer and so seems secure in the respect of the university world.

MacKenzie did not disclaim the celebrity which was thrust upon him and crossed the line which divides consultant from presenter. He defected to the enemy, to the great benefit and enjoyment of millions of viewers, but at some cost to his academic reputation.

In less embattled areas of television where culture prevails over controversy, Kenneth Clark's 'Civilisation' and Jacob Bronowski's 'The Ascent of Man', with some support from General Sir Brian Horrocks on military matters, blazed a trail down which David Attenborough and Jonathan Miller strode. In a more severely expository mode, straight-to-camera utterance with a minimum of supporting props,

Patrick Moore on astronomy and A. J. P. Taylor on modern history have made a great impact.

The sheer sumptuousness of documentary series such as 'Life on Earth', the exotic locations and the brilliant exploitation of technical effects seemed to disarm many of the traditional enemies of television, who were prepared to concede, however grudgingly, that the medium had at last done something not wholly despicable. Of course, the ideas dealt with were rarely abstract in the strict sense. They were usually incarnate within a rich vein of visual material, and often carried by a strong historical narrative.

The only television pundit of any note in the religious field was the late Dr William Barclay, and most of his programmes were made in and for Scotland rather than the UK network. There is a curious tradition which goes a long way back in religious broadcasting that it is a Bad Thing to encourage the cult of the television personality. This notion is at odds with the practice in all other forms of television. Oddly, it is more fervently canvassed by some clerics who have been familiar since their theological college days with that definition of preaching as truth mediated through personality.

The tradition of religious television anonymity has its origin in pre-war radio days when the Revd W. H. Elliott, Rector of St Michael's, Chester Square, broadcast every week for five years. Not only did he become that dreaded thing, a religious cult figure, but conventional wisdom has it that he had a breakdown through trying to cope with listeners' requests for pastoral help. It is said that the sheer volume of human misery broke his heart.

William Barclay's programmes which had a tremendous vogue in Scotland for over eight years were more a brilliant defiance of the medium of television than a creative use of it. They were usually expositions of the Bible done in a style halfway between that of the lecture room and the pulpit. Barclay used no props and scorned studio tricks. He carried the programmes by his genius for illustrating sound scholarship with popular anecdote. It was the classical Scottish preacher's gift.

There was one thing in particular about William Barclay which television latched on to. He was a 'character' with a rasping voice, not overly pretty face and a hearing-aid. And he was an enthusiast for his subject – a quality the medium captures and magnifies.

William Barclay was not an intellectual in the generally accepted sense. He did not play around with ideas. He was firmly within the story-telling tradition of Christianity, yet according to Ronnie Falconer, the BBC's religious broadcasting chief in Scotland who discovered him, he attracted much abuse from fellow academics and some Church of Scotland divines. That proportion of vilification which was not inspired by jealousy seems to have had a class aspect – radio is refined but television is vulgar and theological professors ought to have nothing to do with it.

The Innate Resistance of the Medium
Not all intellectuals are Luddite in their attitude to television. Some, as we have seen, approach it positively, put themselves to school with television professionals and study the private language of the medium. They are eager to sell their ideas within the largest market-place in the history of the world. Yet the medium itself seems to resist them.

Television has a preoccupation, almost an obsession, with achieving and holding the largest possible audience. Indeed, a television network, whether financed by advertising or licence fee, can survive only if it is able to count its programme viewers in millions.

This appetite for mass audiences is not necessarily fuelled by greed, though understandably advertisers want to reach the biggest market they can. The reason some very clever men and women enter the broadcasting industry is because they relish the intellectual challenge of giving the generality of society the Reithian gifts of entertainment, enlightenment and information. Because the mass media audience cannot be known to the broadcaster, he acquires a catholicity of taste which wars with minority programming and specialised subjects.

No idea can be addressed to the generality of society, unless it is so summary as to be more a sentiment than a concept. It used to be said of the politician who wished to please everybody and avoid controversy that he was against sin and for motherhood. Now both sin and motherhood are contentious audience-dividing issues.

It is part of the changing nature of discourse in our society, for which the mass media are chiefly responsible, that people no longer form publics, though they may belong to pressure groups concerned to push sectional demands. Hence, serious ideas must be aimed with sniper-like precision; they cannot be scattered like shotgun pellets in the general direction of the public.

Front-line thinkers doing pioneering work are chiefly concerned to address other thinkers who can appreciate the novelty of the scholarship because they know what has been thought before. Television is an absurdly inefficient way of reaching such an audience.

The shape of the television programme militates against the communication of serious ideas. Programmes are tightly packaged according to the producer's perception of the viewer's attention-span. The movement or flow of the action is rapid, there is no possibility of digressing or entering qualifications about the main theme. One or two points must be made in a clear and vivid manner. The nuances integral to structured thought are excluded. And the package must be tied up in ribbon and delivered as a finished product before the theme music of the next programme is heard on the stroke of scheduled time.

Most important of all, television as a medium for the communication of ideas cannot offer its viewers any time for reflection. It is a sequential medium in which episode follows remorselessly upon episode. At no point can the viewer cry halt and ask for something to be repeated. He is required to absorb meaning at the speed of light, literally.

The fact that viewers are offered no reflection time is not inherent to the medium. The action *could* be slowed down, but the idea of 'flow' – the sweep from one programme half-hour to the next – is deeply ingrained in a public tutored by television for a quarter of a century. Any slackening of pace seems unutterably tedious.

If one is denied the leisure to reflect upon serious ideas, it is difficult to see in what way they can actually be understood. The greater availability of home video-cassette recorders and the establishment of some élite subscription cable television not wedded to the concept of mass audiences may change all this. But for the moment, the networks are where it is all happening. And the conundrum remains.

Television is a visual medium, so what about ideas for which no visual material exists? Here is an excellent example offered by Jerry Kuehl, who produced 'The World at War' for Thames Television:

> The relations between Church and State were very important to the leaders of the Third Reich, and, it goes without saying, to ordinary Germans too. But very little film was ever made which even showed National Socialist leaders and churchmen together, let alone doing anything significant. *So considerations of Church and State were virtually omitted from our films on Nazi Germany – and from our commentary.*[19]

The fact that a particular piece of film is unobtainable determines the way a snatch of history is portrayed on the television screen by many producers. There *are* other methods by which dealings between the Third Reich and the German Church could have been described – interviews with survivors, still photography, direct address to camera. But archive film is felt to have a special kind of authority.

In reality, archive film such as a newsreel or early movie documentary has been edited by *someone*. It is not a natural raw ingredient which inevitably adds to the authenticity of the modern documentary. The film has been subject to the same or comparable constraints and distortions as present-day material, but two generations back.

The question whether there is visual material to illustrate a thesis is crucial to the way ideas are dealt with on television. It may even determine whether they are dealt with at all. For instance, other things being equal, viewers of religious television are more likely to get a documentary on the theology of Karl Barth than the theology of John Calvin.

The producer is not making any value judgments about the importance of the one rather than the other. Karl Barth happened to live on into a time when his image and words could be captured on film. The footage is to hand.

There is something cannibalistic about television; it feeds off itself, recycling its old products and offering them as supporting material for the new. And the streaky, black and white film of yesterday, whose subjects move in a comically jerky manner because the original was cranked at sixteen frames a second, has the stamp of the real. What documents are to the historian, actuality footage is to the film producer – proof that something actually happened and in a certain way. The notion is debatable.

Thus, even when there is visual material to support and illustrate an idea, the value of this corroboration needs to be assessed. And who validates the material? Television has its own breed of philosopher-kings who pronounce upon the truth of ideas.

Star-Power

In the Age of Television, authority is vested in a new breed of philosopher-kings (and queens) whose power is in the simple fact of their celebrity. The endorsement by a celebrity of a product or an idea or an ideal assures mass acceptance. As John Phelan puts it:

> If a celebrity is a celebrity because he is celebrated, an opinion is persuasive, an idea is important, an ideal is worthy because it is endorsed by a celebrity. In a way, the celebrity invests the things related to him with, not surprisingly, celebrity.
> To produce a movie, get a star. To cure diseases, get a star. To sell soap, get a star. To save a soul, get a star. To be heard, be a star.[20]

So comedians raise funds for medical research because Nobel Prize winners in medicine do not carry the same conviction with viewers. TV actors and actresses are drafted in to endorse US Presidential aspirants when the candidate himself does not seem able to get across to the public.

Organisers of public events from school fêtes through

supermarket openings to church anniversaries now look to stars to bring in the crowds. Once it was the great preachers who packed the pews on special occasions; now a television actor with a minor part in 'Coronation Street' may well be a bigger draw than the Archbishop or Moderator or Chief Rabbi.

The performance of media pundits such as Kenneth Clark and Jacob Bronowski may seem to be a million miles removed from the crudities of the television-star system at its most strident. They surely had the inherent authority of great knowledge of their particular subjects and were acknowledged as experts in the circles that matter long before their faces appeared on the screen. This is so, yet the medium has a way of superimposing its own version of authority even upon the undoubted expert.

Here is a shrewd if sour comment on the matter from Colin McArthur, a Marxist television theorist:

> Dr Bronowski, in the space of one programme, may be seen on the Icelandic coast, in his California home, on Easter Island and in the Caves of Altamira... John Kenneth Galbraith may be spirited from Edinburgh via Paris to Quebec. This locating of the narrator in the actual substance of his narration offers a quasi-talismanic guarantee of truth: the *place* actually exists, therefore what is said is true. This has nothing to do with *history* and everything to do with *television*. What we are seeing is television – and specifically the well-financed co-production series – displaying its resources.[21]

There is enough truth in this comment to make any sensitive television producer uncomfortable. If there is no other way of validating an idea, then the willingness to spend large sums of money filming in locations associated with it is a means of underwriting its importance.

The year 1983 was the five-hundredth anniversary of the birth of Martin Luther. Not even television has the power to reincarnate the great Reformer and to interview him about his feelings and reactions when by accident he created Protestantism. But it can be confidently assumed that television cameras prowled around Mansfeld, Erfurt, Worms, Wartburg and Wittenberg – to mention some of the places associated with Luther's life and work.

Presenters, some of them reputable Luther scholars, said their piece in these hallowed places. They could have made identical statements outside Barnsley Town Hall or the Neasden Palais de Dance and the location would not in the least have affected the truth of what they were saying. But if the media pundit discusses the ninety-five theses on the site of the Schlosskirche at Wittenberg his words will carry a special authority because he is *there*.

This, of course, is a gigantic non-sequitur. But it is the nature of television to confer authority on ideas by second-hand visual association.

The role of a narrator becomes crucial when an idea is elusive and the illustrative material is meagre or not totally convincing. He elucidates the idea and guides the viewer through the image sequences. So familiar are we with this convention of the narrator either as a disembodied voice or a figure wandering through the landscape that we often do not notice the extent to which he modifies the idea not only by what he says but by who he is. I say 'he' advisedly. Unless a programme has an overtly feminist theme, it is highly unlikely a woman's voice will be used.

The narrator's tone of voice can decisively change the nature of the idea being spelt out. For instance, footage of the 1926 General Strike with a voice-over commentary spoken in the orotund Churchillian tones of Robert Hardy may put a quite different slant on what is seen from the same words spoken by an actor with a Cockney or Geordie or Glaswegian accent. The one may underline the official version of events while the other is ironic and subversive of them.

The devices which must be used to overcome the innate resistance of the medium to ideas themselves add to the complexities of the problem. Trying to get the medium to do what does not come naturally to it can be subversive of the integrity of the very ideas being promoted.

Talking Heads Versus Moving Pictures

Someone quoted at Leo Rosten, the humorist, the popular saying, 'A picture is worth a thousand words.' He retorted, 'Draw me a picture of Lincoln's Gettysburg Address!' Conventional wisdom has it that radio rather than television should be used to communicate ideas that cannot easily be visualised. The studio discussion, dismissively described in the trade as 'radio with pictures' or 'talking heads' is sometimes seen as a compromise between the two media, radio and TV.

The studio discussion is discounted by some television producers for a number of reasons. Television is about *action*, they claim, and talking heads are static. Nothing happens but chat; the discussion could just as easily be held on the telephone. The narrative strength of television is not employed in a discussion programme and no resolution of an issue is possible other than through the chairman's summing-up.

In a burst of frankness, some producers will confess that they prefer the film documentary treatment of a subject to that of a studio discussion because they have absolute control over a film operation at each stage. If the first attempt at filming doesn't work, the sequence can be shot again because film stock is comparatively cheap. Then, in the cutting room, the film will be edited to the producer's satisfaction, to make the precise points he or she thinks important. Finally, when the commentary is added the narrative thread can be sewn up tightly – words and pictures perfectly matched.

On the other hand, a studio discussion, if it is live, has an element of unpredictability about it which the film producer finds worrying. He or she cannot control narrative flow. Speakers digress, lose the point or leave an idea hanging in the air. Chairmen are too dominant or too permissive. It all adds up to the possibility of a messy, inconclusive programme which offends the producer's sense of order. Nor is he or she likely to be taxed technically. Studio direction of a discussion programme is usually comparatively straightforward, though it is an exacting art when done properly.

Yet this is one obvious way of dealing with abstract ideas – to get them articulated by an expert or opinionated speaker and challenged by others. Nor do talking heads, by definition, make boring television. It depends who they are, what they are saying and the way they interact with other speakers.

Champions of the talking-heads school of television would argue that pictures can be distracting as well as illuminating. A producer may be sorely tempted to show interesting pictures at any cost and so trivialise an argument in order to make a theme viewable. Here is the master of the studio discussion format, Sir Robin Day, defending the concept of talking-head television:

> I have come to feel strongly that television, which has such an enormous power to project violence and unreason, should do more to present reasoned and civilised argument which is the basis of our democratic system. The electronic journalism of television must do more than transmit bloody good pictures.[22]

He goes on to argue for the 'live' talking-head type programme as an event which ought to bring out the best in the performers because adrenalin is flowing freely:

> In a (studio discussion) the main point is that it is a once-for-all affair. There is no repetition, no editing. Timing must be exact. It is a 'live' performance with the feeling of a vast audience watching. Reactions are heightened by the sense of occasion. Mental processes are at their pitch of concentration. The performance is usually fresher, warmer, more spontaneous than it would be on film.

That is an impressive endorsement. However, it would not be unfair to comment that Robin Day is attracted to the genre for precisely the same reason a documentary film producer prefers his or her own chosen medium – the ability to shape and control what happens. What separates them is Robin Day's preference for the more hazardous art of creating order out of spontaneity and unpredictability live on the screen rather than in the less fraught atmosphere of the cutting room.

Whether or not viewers find studio discussion of ideas more interesting than a documentary-style treatment of them is, I suspect, very much a matter of personal taste. There is also a generation factor – verbal confrontation is a much more acceptable form of discourse for the refugees of literary culture than for the progeny of the television age.

But television still imposes severe constraints even on the talking-head treatment of abstract ideas. Some complex ideas can only be fitted into this electronic Procrustean bed by lopping off their arms and legs. Participants in such discussions frequently confess to a sense of frustration that 'all the talk didn't really get anywhere'.

In his inimitable way, Malcolm Muggeridge parodies talking-head religious television. He knows the genre – for twenty years he dominated it:

> Panels! Dear God, the panels. Seated round the microphone, a professor of sociology from Leeds, a resonant life peeress with a moustache, a nondescript clergyman heavy with sideburns, and myself. 'Do the Panel Think?' Oh we do, we do. Thinkers all![23]

So the talking-heads treatment of ideas on television is apparently not greatly loved by *anybody* – producers, panellists *or* audiences, judging by their modest size. In a media world where camera crews travel to the ends of the earth at vast cost to bring the viewer entertaining programmes, studio discussion is redolent of 'cheap' television, a term which has become synonymous with 'sub-standard' or 'stop-gap'.

On the positive side, one reason why studio discussions are judged to be messy, inconclusive and frustrating to take part in is that they resist more stubbornly than a film documentary does television's tendency to turn ideas into 'issues'. They rarely succeed, but the attempt is to be applauded.

Sleight-of-Hand – Idea into Issue[24]

In the old days, before the mass media changed the nature of public discourse, the term 'issue' had a commonly accepted meaning. An issue was a matter of public concern which could be sharpened up by debate until a number of alternative policies emerged. Protagonists held different opinions about these policy options but argued from the basis of a common system of values.

On the television screen, issues are ways of packaging information rather than matters of moment. They are not questions to be thought through, but things one ought to know about; what the television producer has a duty to bring to our attention. In a word, issues are *topics*, items on the television agenda which pop up again and again to provoke argument, controversy and outrage.

Once upon a time, issues were resolved by hard thought, tough policy decisions and the passing of time. Issues on television are not sharpened and resolved but become generalised into attitudes about life – peace and war, crime and punishment, unemployment and inflation. These dichotomies are easily perceived by viewers to be sharply opposed, but they are also too vast to do much about.

The television issue is like a perpetual glowing ember waiting to be fanned into flame by the gusts of topical controversy – the multiple murder raises yet again the issue of crime and punishment or public order; an assassination attempt revives once more the issue of public security; an opinion poll finding invites renewed speculation about the issue of the Labour Party leadership.

One reason why viewers love 'issues' is because they inevitably spark off a ritual combat between television personalities. This they find entertaining, a painless way of dealing with but not disposing of a serious matter. Television issues have more in common with sport than with serious current affairs. They are occasions for contests in which no one finally wins or loses because the teams clash again and again.

We are back to the business of *broad*casting again – attracting and holding the attention of mass audiences. The more specific an idea is, the further it can be taken by sustained reasoning towards some resolution but the fewer the people whose interest will be engaged. Issues are vast bran tubs into which the generality of the public can dip and bring out something that interests them.

The essence of mass marketing is that the same product can be repeated endlessly. So it is with television issues. If they were actually resolved, there would be long periods when the television screen was blank. But so long as race riots break out sporadically in this city and that, the Middle East remains volatile, the world economy wallows in recession and apartheid in South Africa persists, the issues of the 'eighties will be paraded before the viewing public and most will live on into the 'nineties.

The public personalities associated with these issues will, on cue, joust like gladiators again and again. These media celebrities can enter the television studios on any one occasion confident that their appearance fees will not dry up. The debaters will not dispose finally and irrevocably of the matter under discussion this time or the next. Television issues are, if not immortal, extremely long-lived.

Consider the persistence of the television issue as it affects one media-star, Mr Enoch Powell. He is, of course, the race specialist. He might therefore expect to be invited to air his views on television if any one of a number of eventualities sparks off the perennial race issue – riots, allegations of racial discrimination in public or private institutions, crime statistics broken down into racial categories and so on. Incidents come and go, the issue marches on, endlessly discussed but never resolved.

I am not suggesting that serious discussion about television issues is impossible. Plainly, there *is* good talk on television. Verbal battle often begins in the studio or on film about matters of moment and is then continued next day in the home, at the bus stop or the place of employment.

Television issues stimulate debate, argument and comment. But they are seldom spurs to action because it is precisely at the point where they harden into specific policy options that the generality of viewers lose interest. And television professionals have highly developed antennae which warn them when viewers are no longer with them.

So if the presumption is that theological ideas are not matters for idle speculation but should lead to action in worship, mission or service, then television is not a promising medium through which to communicate them. They will be degutted, turned into issues and added to a very long agenda for periodic airing and inconclusive debate.

PART THREE

CHRISTIAN STRATEGY IN THE TELEVISION AGE

NINE

Electronic Babel – the Zone of Mission

As I have tried to argue, we are living through the last afternoon of the Dark Ages of the Electronic Era, poised on the lip of change that might soberly be described as cataclysmic. Doing theology on the side of a mountain in a howling gale just as the avalanche starts is an exhilarating experience, but any conclusions reached should be treated with caution.

Nor should we forget that it is the Church's task to evolve strategies of mission. This is a cumbersome, messy and slow way of doing things, but God willed it so by vesting authority and wisdom not in talented individualists but in fallible collectivisms – tribe, people and fellowship. Waspish geniuses have cavorted about during Christian history like agile dogs yapping at the heels of the moving caravan; their proper role is to sting, provoke and stimulate the Church, not to short-circuit it.

One definition of theology is disciplined reflection on the action of the people of God – first the action, then the reflection. So Christians will have to thrash around in uncharted waters for some time before they learn much worth knowing about effective witness in the Television Age.

The best I can do is draw attention to themes I believe the Church needs to consider urgently. What follows is an agenda rather than a report. Many of these themes originate in areas of human enquiry of which I have no specialised knowledge. It is for the scholars to develop or dispose of them as the search for truth dictates.

Willed But Not Fated

I begin with a self-directed warning. Television is such an inherently dramatic invention that even writing about it tends to heat the blood and it is easy to be carried away on clouds of hyperbole. *Babel* will serve as a metaphor for the ultimate information explosion and its consequences, provided one keeps one's feet on the ground and avoids elevating television to the status of a technological divinity. The god with the unwinking eye which has its temple in the corner of the room may have immense power but it is not irresistible.

The notion of the machine as god goes back a long way. In 1900 Henry Adams, the American writer, visited the Great Exposition in Paris and spent the summer watching the giant dynamos in the Champ de Mars. To him they were symbols of divinity. He wrote, 'I begin to feel the forty-foot dynamo as a moral force, much as early Christians felt the Cross. Before the end one began to pray to it.' He even composed a poem addressing one of these fearsome new inventions in extravagant terms:

> Mysterious Power! Gentle Friend!
> Despotic Master! Tireless Force!
> What are we then? The Lords of Space?
> The master-mind whose tasks you do?
> Or are we atoms whirled apace
> Shaped and controlled by you?[25]

Lewis Mumford, the social planner and visionary, felt that in an age which had abandoned its historic symbols, especially those of traditional religion, the machine seemed to be the only symbol left with universal validity. Substitute 'television' for 'machine' and this comment identifies a heresy around whose edges I have been tiptoeing throughout the book. It is the notion of television as the source of a form of technological determinism – a machine which has become a monster, generating a life and direction of its own, independent of human agency, fated to assume mastery because of its irresistible power.

Back to the machine as god. The arch-apostle of technological determinism, Marshall McLuhan, romanticised
television to the point where it seemed to be an almost
mystical force. He attributed to it the powers that Henry
Adams once claimed for the dynamo. In Raymond
William's[26] view, McLuhan turned a number of interesting
though doubtful artistic opinions into an all-embracing
social theory. He talked and wrote about television as
though it were the sufficient, single cause of the modern age,
reducing all other causes, including all that people have
classified as history, to effects.

The very term 'medium' has a vague abstract ring to it and
permits all kinds of expansive speculation unhampered by
the need to take account of hard facts. McLuhan's belief in
television as the cause actually had the effect of abolishing
history in the sense of real times and places in favour of a
generalised environment, an ideal essence, a sort of metaphysical mist like the vapour which, according to one
theory, cooled down to produce the universe.

McLuhan's most famous aphorism, 'The Medium is the
Message', when seen from this viewpoint is actually a
manifesto for the totalitarian rule of the machine. If the bare
existence of the medium is self-justifying, regardless of the
messages it conveys, then the human contribution to
television becomes peripheral except in strictly service and
maintenance terms. The content of television is as otiose as a
slogan chalked on the casing of a high explosive shell – the
missile is its own deafening eloquence.

The deification of television is just an ancient heresy
decked out in ultra-modern dress – the notion of the future
being shaped by a blind force with random consequences
rather than by the work of the human will through intention
and struggle. The Christian would wish to challenge this
heresy at an even more fundamental level. Neither the
meaning the person finds in history (blind force) nor the
meaning he imposes on history (human will) is sufficient to
explain its drama, which is being worked out in a frame of
meaning too grand for human beings to comprehend let
alone manage effectively.

It is not necessary, however, to invoke the Christian doctrine of history to contest the notion that the nature of a whole society could depend upon the fixed properties of something called television. For like 'medium', the word 'television' is shorthand for a whole collection of things, it is the label on a rag-bag of miscellaneous concepts, properties, attitudes and devices. It is not a monolith like a huge boulder crashing down the mountain-side.

For instance, between television as invention and television as technology a bewildering array of human agencies and forces have their effect. Scientific, military, commercial and political pressure groups and interests all clamour for a share in shaping it. It did not spring from the ground fully armed when some latter-day Cadmus called Logie Baird sowed dragons' teeth. Television is a process, subject to cultural and social definition. It cannot be defined in some grand philosophical sweep as a distant first cause from which all else that goes on in the electronic Babel is a necessary effect.

Our perception of television is complex for while it may be true that it is not the single cause of the tensions and demands of the electronic society, many of the other causes are identified, made visible and mediated to the public through the small screen. Because television puts its own gloss on whatever it transmits, these other causes appear to be related to and affected by the medium. Thus it assumes a false dominance in some hierarchy of forces moulding the new Babel.

In essence, this section is a plea that we should avoid the error of seeking to understand television in terms of any one-dimensional definition. Above all, we must not allow it to become the source and inspiration of some crude, deterministic theology. Like all the works of our hands and minds and imaginations, it is an extension of human dominion over the earth.

As a secular institution, television is outside the control of the Church in a way some of the earlier communication media were not. But this is not to say that it is outside the range of God's sovereignty or Man's dominion. Human beings have willed it into existence but they are not fated to be its victims. The mastery of it is theirs, and they dare not forget the fact.

The Ultimate Open Society

This will be the distinctive social feature of the Television Age. Sociologists use the terms 'open' and 'closed' in a special sense. According to Edmund Carpenter,[27] a closed society is one in which there is a tight correlation between information and behaviour. In the true closed society there is virtually no superfluous information about; most of what is available is put to use and acted upon. In an open society there is enough information available to its members to form the basis for a number of alternative courses of action.

Once the electronic gadgetry of the Television Age is in place an information explosion will portend the ultimate open society. Individual citizens will be bombarded by information from so many sources and on so many subjects that the link between knowing and acting is likely to be severed. Very little of this tidal wave of information will be serviceable to us.

As though this were not enough, advertising men, who have to pay for every split second of radio or television time they use, are trying to pack even more information into a given time-span. Code-words that trigger off a whole succession of ideas are dinned into our consciousness and in months become common currency where once it took decades or even centuries for words to be added to the popular vocabulary.

And in sheer self-defence, those citizens who are sinking from sight under a stream of packaged information are trying to increase their ability to cope by taking courses in speed-writing and rapid-reading. Split-screen and multi-screen presentations are now appearing in some public places such as airports, hurling multiple images at us simultaneously. The corporate metabolism of our society is having to speed up in order to survive an information-saturated environment.

This cataract of engineered messages which sweeps over

the citizen has the baleful effect of blocking out the natural messages we once derived from the world about us. We can no longer 'hear' and 'read' nature. Engineered messages are only intelligible when they are decoded according to social conventions painstakingly acquired. The ears of the citizen of the Television Age will be attuned to the nuances of a wide range of manufactured information codes but are likely to filter out the primary language of creation.

How have citizens of Western society learned to cope with the information glut of the open society? By a philosophical device first described by Bertrand Russell – the technique of the suspended judgment. Overwhelmed by the sheer volume of messages coming at us from all sides, we do not reject most of the information nor do we act upon it. It flows over and through us and we accept it without making it the basis of our life-style. We suspend judgment on its practical significance.

This learned passivity has a physiological as well as philosophical component. Sir John Eccles, the Nobel Prize-winning neurologist, in an article in *Scientific American* has argued that the least understood and most vital function of the human brain is its ability to resist messages which pour in faster than it can cope. The technical term for this power of blocking off is inhibition. It is essential to sanity because it prevents overload and cerebral fuse-blowing.

People who have developed the knack of dealing with information by suspending judgment about it present a formidable challenge to Christian mission. They become the floating voters of politics, the 'don't knows' of social surveys and non-combatants in moral crusades. How then will the Gospel, which demands decision, fare when it is heard as one message among many others by people who have been trained to suspend judgment upon most of what they hear and see?

Avery Dulles, the American theologian, comments that the electronic media are resistant to imposed patterns of dogmatic religion and quotes William Kuhns:

The entertainment milieu has transformed the ways in which

we believe and are capable of believing. An absolute kind of belief, as well as a belief in absolutes, becomes increasingly difficult as the entertainment milieu trains people to believe tentatively and with elasticity... the very concept of faith – to believe in that which you cannot see and cannot understand – comes with difficulty to a generation which has depended, as perhaps no generation before, on its sense...[28]

Dulles, pondering this quotation, wonders whether faith is still possible for those whose psyche has been predominantly formed by the image industry. These citizens of the Television Age are so conscious of the subtle techniques of manipulation that they spontaneously disbelieve much of what they see.

The Gospel is still heard with clarity and urgency within the community of faith. Believers are attuned to its distinctive nuances and competing messages are excluded. The religious environment is still a verbal and literary one which accords well with the expression of the Word in speech and music and silence.

But how intelligible will the Gospel be when addressed to society in the Television Age? It is bound to come across as just another highly engineered message, and one which requires decoding, however much Christians insist it is universally accessible. In the ultimate open society, will a message originating in pastoral Palestine two millennia ago have such luminous meaning that it can strike home in spite of its antiquely rhetorical style – *and* in competition with countless other messages expressed in the contemporary visual idiom?

Those Christians who rely absolutely on the Holy Spirit to overleap cultural gaps and make the old, old story plain to everyone, everywhere, in every age, mock all talk about suspended judgment and neurological inhibition. They call it faithlessness. However, the evidence is against them. Writes Dennis Nineham at the outset of a closely reasoned argument about Biblical inspiration:

If there is to be divine communication to men who dwell in history, it will inevitably be historically conditioned... If it is to be intelligible to those to whom it is made, it will have to be in terms of their institutions, assumptions and myths, which means that it will have to be in culturally conditioned terms. *There is no possibility of a revelation which transcends culturally conditioned terms altogether and is given in terms which are not peculiar to any one culture but apply equally to all cultures.*[29]

American strategists of mission, rarely reluctant to add to the jargon, talk about *dynamic equivalence* and *adaptive orientation* as methods of trying to bridge cultural gaps in communication. Dynamic equivalence looks to the receiving culture for myths, legends or facts which correspond to Biblical ideas. The missionary, besides being a keen linguist, becomes an assiduous collector of folklore and proverb.

Adaptive orientation is about ways of allowing the receiving culture to shape the Christian message. This is a risky enterprise, eschewed by more conservative missionaries who fear for the integrity of the Gospel. But the aim is to avoid subjecting someone to the pressures of Western culture as the price of learning Christian truth.

The challenge to Christian communication of bridging cultural gaps between, say, the West and Africa and Asia is now well recognised, fully documented and carefully studied in missionary training courses. It is, however, arguable that so all-pervasive is the mass of information now flooding our own society, we are dealing not with a cultural gap between Television Age and those which preceded it but with the total disintegration of 'culture' as the term has traditionally been understood.

Can any individual or group comprehend enough of the vast tide of contemporary knowledge to construct a universally or even generally accepted meaning-system from it all? Dame Helen Gardner, writing from the very heart of academic orthodoxy, puts it this way:

We live today in a world where the immense extensions of knowledge in every sphere have made a synthesis of our knowledge into anything that could be called a 'world view' impossible... It is difficult to believe that any future scholars will ever attempt to construct a systematic picture of common beliefs and assumptions for the twentieth century.

The strategists of Christian mission must therefore conjure with the fact that in the Television Age, many people do not reject Christianity in favour of other claims upon their allegiance, but are so bewildered by all the options open to them, many of them unstructured, that they find any choice beyond them. They suspend judgment and walk quickly past the great gaggle of street-corner messiahs bawling their wares in the electronic market-place.

The effect of large numbers of members of our society declaring themselves spiritual non-combatants is seen in the decline of mass evangelism. The great rhetorical skills and immense dedication poured into classical evangelical proclamation warm the hearts of the faithful, bring home the half-converted wanderer and entice some on the fringes of ecclesiastical culture to draw nearer the centre.

These are laudable aims, and it is an important part of Christian mission to pursue them. But the truth is that the generality of the population are unmoved by classical evangelical rhetoric (some would claim they always have been) even when amplified by electronic gadgetry. The days are long gone when the preacher could address the pew and the market-place in the same language.

The Gospel was first proclaimed in a closed society. Other than village gossip, there was probably very little alternative intelligence to preoccupy the minds of ordinary people. It was not hard to see the link between what they heard and how they ought to behave. 'Go, and do thou likewise' might promise great hardship but the injunction was plain, practical and unmuted by a clangour of siren-voices.

Seventeen hundred years later, the Evangelical Revival occurred in a society which was still not open. Wesley's itinerant preachers carried messages much of whose secular power lay in the fact that they put hearers in isolated communities in touch with truths exciting the minds of others beyond the parish boundaries.

Methodists justifiably boast about the extraordinary

distances covered each year on horseback by John Wesley in the course of his preaching. These vast mileages testify not only to Wesley's stamina and zeal but also to the extent that eighteenth-century Britain was still a closed society. Dennis Nineham quotes Valery to the effect that the Paris-Toulouse journey took 200 hours in Roman times; two thousand years later in 1750, the stage-coach still could not do the journey in under 160 hours.

It is obvious that speed of communication is the single most important catalyst of social and cultural change. Hence, for the first time in the history of Christianity the Gospel will have to take its chance in the ultimate open society. This could well be the final frontier of mission.

Television. Ritual and Icon[30]

Even the citizens of the electronic Babel must find ways of giving meaning to their lives and of expressing their sense of what meaning is through public symbols. Human behaviour patterns have always been shaped in part by the power of the imagination working itself out in stories, models, symbols and images. In this way, people have located themselves in the universe, in society and in their own heads.

Certain archetypal themes run through the life and experience of everyone in every age. They do not disappear when particular symbols for expressing them become evacuated of meaning; the imagination seeks others.

For instance, when the myths and symbols which the Churches offer to explain these archetypal themes lose potency for all but their own members, the spirit-life of society does not thereby wither. The unbeliever's life is still touched by dread and glory – fears have to be subdued, order imposed on experience and some sort of response made to the ultimate questions of life and death. There is a perennial search for effective symbols which make sense of this struggle.

Television is the most potent source of myth and symbol for increasing numbers of people. It weaves a web of accessible imagery which those outside the charmed circle of formal religion can draw on to feed the life of the spirit. And it provides public symbols around which fragmented groups and individuals can cohere.

There is, for example, television's role in meeting people's deep need for ritual. Ritual is the ceremonial re-enactment of the stories by which we live, especially those about our origins and destiny. By imposing order on an untidy, unpredictable and frightening world, ritual directs the human being into the flow of sacred power in the way iron filings line up in response to a magnetic field.

It is fascinating to see how television shapes up to the demands of the basic elements of ritual. Ritual takes place in a sacred space, set apart from the routine spaces of ordinary life. Sacred space may be contained within an elaborate architectural edifice like a cathedral or be bare ground marked by the graves of the gods and ancestors as in African tribal society. But the space is set apart, specially ordered to make communion possible.

Ritual-time is also sacred. It is not measured by the clock but forms a carefully structured cohesive unity which has a beginning a middle and an end. In ordinary life we are always in the midst of the 'now' – a time-flow whose beginnings have slipped far behind us and whose climax is shrouded in uncertainty. In ritual-time, we can project ourselves both backwards and forwards to contemplate our origins and destiny.

The core of all ritual is the story of a crucial event considered so important that it generates loyalty and faith in those who hear it. This event may really have happened or be legendary, but in the act of recalling it, all its original potency is released and the participant returns to the everyday world with renewed vigour and confidence.

So a ritual act involves us in withdrawing from the ordinary world into a special space, time and action. In *Myth and Reality*, Mircea Eliade says that by means of ritual the believer is 'tirelessly conquering the world, organising it, transforming the landscape of nature into a cultural milieu.'[31] This is precisely what television does – it transforms a landscape of images into a cultural milieu, thus performing a ritual act.

Television operates in a special space. The screen is a window opening on to a world which has its own private existence and yet entices viewers to enter because it mirrors the world they are familiar with. And television-time is special time. Thanks to the satellite, time-zones are abolished, today and tomorrow coalesce in the urgent 'now' of the television programme seen simultaneously from one side of the world to the other.

Occasionally, there is the clash of sacred spaces and times like the struggle of contending gods – Pope John Paul II's visit to Britain happened on a Whitsun weekend when the calendar was bursting with sporting events. Television did the visit proud, showing live transmissions of the Pope's triumphal progress for hours on end. But sometimes his itinerary fell behind schedule and television programmes overran, keeping sports fans waiting for their favourite events. The BBC and Independent Television companies were inundated with telephone calls of protest – the pontiff had invaded the sacred space of sports fans and taken up some of their hallowed time.

There is a pseudo-liturgical rhythm to television time which marks it off from the patterns of everyday living. There are fixed points at which viewers keep tryst with their television sets – seven-thirty on Mondays and Wednesdays means 'Coronation Street' for seventeen million viewers a week. And at nine o'clock on the BBC or ten o'clock in ITV people keep in touch with the nation and outside world by tuning in to the news, which is a public symbol through which one version of reality can be understood.

Because television is an electronic story-teller whose fishy eye is always on the look out for spectacle, events when televised assume a high symbolic significance. The wedding of Prince Charles and Lady Diana Spencer, watched by an estimated eleven thousand million viewers throughout the world came across as the richly symbolic fable of the prince and the virgin. Winston Churchill's televised funeral had Wagnerian overtones as the old warrior was sped on his way to Valhalla, loaded with honours. And millions of Americans wept openly as they watched the funeral of John

F. Kennedy, the resplendent hero struck down at the height of his powers by a malign fate.

Such momentous events would be matters of public record in any epoch, but television allowed ordinary people a sense of participation in the actual occasion which they could never have known through newspaper accounts or history books. Though it might be claimed there are no compensations for physical presence at a great occasion, television is able to communicate aspects of visual splendour and intimacy that elude the actual spectator, thanks to multiple cameras with a range which encompasses both panorama and close-up.

It is not just great events to which television gives powerfully symbolic significance. Any event framed by the small screen and happening in special space and time has a ritual aspect. And the television ritual by allowing the mass sharing of stories and events at a uniform time is a major force for social integration. The flow of electronic signals affects the way people think collectively not only about serious matters but also about the froth of life such as fashion, gossip and play.

If television's ritual role is concerned with the action on the screen, what about the images themselves? Here television operates as an icon. Every image is a small segment of experience made visible and turned into an object of contemplation. The icon is a special form of image designed to bring the observer into a special relationship with some sacred power.

I don't want to get ensnared in the long-running theological controversy between the Eastern and Western traditions about the precise significance of icons. The Orthodox icon is not simply a representation of, say, the countenance of Christ, the Virgin or some saint; it is a true epiphany, a self-made imprint charged with supernatural power. In the West, most Catholics and Protestants find the use of sacred images acceptable to stimulate thought, emotion and recollection about the Holy so long as wonder-working power is not attributed to them.

I would place only the most modest and austere

interpretation on the term icon when using it as an analogue
of the ways television is able to communicate contemporary
belief systems and values through the small screen. To my
knowledge, enrapt viewers rarely kiss the television screen
even when the most winsome star is performing, and no
healing miracles have yet been notified to the BBC.
Nevertheless, the notion of television as an icon is a valuable
one.

Traditionally, the icon was a visual explanation of some
kind of symbolic order which helped believers to make sense
of the everyday world. It provided a context within which the
faithful could locate their own present experiences. And it
was a visual metaphor of the eternal, heavenly order,
offering a glimpse of the glories of the world to come in the
midst of a transitory and often painful earthly existence.

The saints and heroes portrayed on icons served not only
as encouragers to the faithful but as models of behaviour.
There was the aspect of a visual catechism to some icons.
They were a checklist of virtues and vices, rewards and
punishments graphically depicted in tableaux about the
divine response to human sinfulness.

So, if the function of an icon were to be loosely defined as
articulating and shaping beliefs through visual forms, it
follows that this can be done just as powerfully by secular as
sacred images. And the most evocative secular images of our
time presented before the maximum number of people for
the longest periods are furnished by television.

Many of these televisual images are admittedly superficial,
even trivial, representations of *anything,* yet the very
pervasiveness of the medium and the relentless pounding of
the cathode ray tube serves to connect the disparate segments
of our lives in some kind of web of understanding. It may be a
simple, crude system of belief that the television icon
portrays, but as Sir John Seeley said a long time ago, 'Public
opinion is necessarily moulded by a few large plain simple
ideas.'

The television icon endlessly offers visual metaphors
which identify and expound some of these 'large plain
simple ideas' – visions and sentiments widely shared

throughout our society. For instance, there is the *family*, endlessly explored in television drama, comedy and documentary programmes; or *nature* - examined microscopically in science features and panoramically in wild life films; and *technology*, a dominant theme in current affairs, science and drama, with the motor-car chases of crime thrillers and the flashing, multicoloured gadgetry of science fiction and space epics.

Each of these icons incorporates a belief system, even though those responsible for producing them would insist, hand on heart, they seek only to inform and entertain. For example, take the basic theme of the technology icon which makes visible a world sustained by faith in science and human inventiveness. Gregor Goethals contrasts traditional sacred icons with the secular iconography of technology shown on television:

> The heroes and heroines in the sacred icons were portrayed as exceptional human beings, though morally frail; their image witnessed a faith in a divine, transcendent being. The icons of technology, by contrast, portray a gospel that can deliver people from ugliness, age, even death and destruction. Central to the new faith is the belief that human nature is not constant and that people like products, can continually be changed, updated, improved and packaged...

What goes for technology applies equally to the rest of the secular icons which occupy the television screen. They locate the viewer in a system of belief, or rather a number of them since we are simultaneously members of many communities and relate to many icons. And each offers us heroes and heroines whom we may choose as models of behaviour. The consequences can be baleful since television's portrayal of minorities generally and of blacks in particular is decidedly patchy with a pronounced bias towards patronisation. Women don't do too well, either.

It is said that human beings cannot live fully without embracing a cause, some object of devotion and some centre of worth - even if they can find nothing more elevated than their own ego. Well, television offers surrogates for these essential drives of human life and sets them out in iconic form with a richness of imagery that is bright, compelling and makes sense to the ordinary viewer.

The gospel being preached on television may be meretricious but at least it is widely shared and easily accessible. Nor is it completely ignoble. There is a heroic theme running through television which is taken up with challenge, risk and self-transcendence. It may be a mountaineer climbing Everest to the whirr of film cameras, a tail-end batsman with a near-impossible total to get but only a limited number of overs to face, or a politician confronted by a hostile studio audience. The variations are endless, but television does seek to satisfy this deep, primitive human desire to run the gauntlet of fate for glory's sake.

Gregor Goethals quotes Ernest Becker about the human need for play and illusion:

> A human being needs a 'second' world, a world of humanly created meaning, a new reality that one can live, dramatise, nourish one's self in. 'Illusion' means creative play at its highest level. Cultural illusion is a necessary ideology of self-justification, a heroic dimension that is life itself to the symbolic animal.[31]

Becker's point is presumably that if we cannot live happily with any of the traditional religious world-views, we shall create our own 'second' world because we cannot survive without drama, pageant, play and creative fantasy. These things nourish the imagination, tease the spirit and irradiate the soul. If formal religion becomes preoccupied with private and esoteric imagery which is inaccessible to the generality of society, a popular piety will spring up, searching for other ways of expressing faith.

This is what is happening in the electronic Babel. Television is offering at least some satisfaction of the human being's need for ritual and icons. The Churches do not seem to realise this and insist on regarding television simply as a regrettable diversion on the enquirer's road to the nearest ecclesiastical outpost, rather as Victorian teetotallers viewed the wayside pub.

Gregor Goethals puts the challenge bluntly:

> Through what forms are religious traditions currently communicating the really great adventure? Until they can quicken the sensations of risk and challenge that animate the last nineteen seconds of a championship play-off with a goal to go, the illusions of culture will continue to satisfy our need for belonging and wonder. Until institutional religion can excite the serious play of the soul and evoke the fullness of human passion, television will nurture our illusions of heroism and self-transcendence.

The Foreign Policy of Babel

The inhabitants of the original Babel were one people and spoke a single language until God got in on the act and scattered them over the face of the earth. Electronic communications systems are busy putting history or myth into reverse by conferring on the citizens of the new Babel an almost sinister sense of internationalism. This will owe something to growing mutual understanding, but much more to a technologically imposed uniformity.

Here are a few jottings from the notebook of a mythical Babelian diplomat which sketch out some of the international realities with which he would have to live. I have mentioned some of these points elsewhere but it is worth collecting them in one place. The list is not exhaustive; merely an impression of the 'feel' of the global village.

Goldfish-Bowl Wars Leaving nuclear holocaust out of account, the effect of electronic communications on lesser wars is bound to be highly ambiguous. Because there can never again be the one-sided reportage of conflict, the myth of the utterly diabolical enemy will not be so easily sustainable nor can uncomfortable truths be suppressed by fiat in order to whip up national fervour. Neither political nor military overlords will relish fighting wars in a goldfish bowl.[32]

But that's just one side of the equation. On the other hand, the world as portrayed by television is often a mean and violent environment for the human species. From the gunfights of the traditional western to the computer dominated inter-stellar battles of *Star Wars* controlled violence is seen as the necessary response to aggression.

The theatricality of television invests with glamour and excitement the impedimenta of the military world – guns, uniforms, aircraft and the like. Bombs explode in riots of colour; blood is garishly visible; flame, smoke and rubble fill the small screen with raw images. If there is an ideological theme about peace and war underlying television output it must surely be that aggressive behaviour must be affirmed as a response to conflict and that massive force is needed to keep in check the violence of others.

If this is the ethos of Babel, what price the disposition that makes for peace among its citizens?

All Things in the Light Modern spy satellites can read the denomination of a postage stamp from 24,000 miles in the sky. Their infra-red eyes are capable of probing deep beneath the earth and registering the slightest movement or change in its material density. The era of old-fashioned military secrets is over. Gone are the days when convoys of fighting ships sailed by night or in dense fog to surprise a complacent enemy. Armies will never again appear suddenly over the horizon to confound opposing strategists who supposed them to be miles away. Surprises, other than those sprung by suicidal military lunatics, have ceased to be tactical possibilities.

The micro-secret may still be inviolate, though only as a marginal advantage – if We are working on it, so are They. We assume We are months ahead of Them, but those are slim odds on which to gamble the survival of the human race. It must be taken for granted that what We know, They also know. Any other assumption is madness.

One reason why They are likely to know what We know is that communications satellites, by means of which most classified information is passed instantaneously from one point to another, are notoriously leaky. High over the new Babel, opposing satellites are locked, antennae to antennae if not eye-ball to eye-ball reading the secrets of one another's hearts.

In the new Babel, what you don't want the whole world let alone your statutory enemy to know, it is best not to formulate even in the privacy of your own head. Even now they are probably busy boring into your skull from outer space.

The Cancellation of Frontiers To communications satellites winking in the far sky, national frontiers are as insubstantial as dotted lines on a map. The president of IBM has said just that:

> For business purposes, the national frontiers which separate one nation from the next are no more real than the equator. Frontiers are mere ethnic, linguistic and cultural conventions. They do not define the needs of business nor the tendencies of the consumers. The world beyond its original frontiers is not considered any longer as a group of unrelated clients and a potential market for its products, but as an extension of a single market . . .[33]

The multinational corporations determine the desirable size of a market in relation to land masses and population densities, regardless of the political units involved, and then deploy all the apparatus of electronic communications to saturate the area. Latin America is a prime target. Writes Fernando Reyes Matta,

> There are countries in Latin America where illiteracy exceeds 60 per cent of the population. However the mass media act on this population, giving them cultural values, aims in life and models of development whose origin corresponds to a dominating transnational ideology.[34]

The Latin American masses are the targets of a sustained and complex publicity campaign which uses every cultural form from imported TV programmes through advertising and planted newspaper stories to propaganda broadcasts

from Voice of America. Day in and day out a development
structure is being built whose main artefacts are provided by
multinational corporations. The way of life dramatised in
magazines, television soap operas and newspaper advertisements defines a type of social order based on the demands of
the consumer society. Political passivity is achieved by
diverting human energy into the struggle for more material
goods.

In the film *Network*, there is a confrontation between the
television superstar, Beale, and Jenson the president of a
world-wide corporation, CCA. Beale has been trying to use
the medium for patriotic reasons to prevent the Arabs from
buying his television network. Jenson, the high priest of
transnational ideology tells Beale the facts of life about a
world in which national labels are meaningless:

> There are no nations! There are no peoples!
> There are no Russians! There are no Arabs!
> There are no Third Worlds! There is no West!
> There is only one holistic system of systems, one vast
> interwoven, interacting, multivariate, multinational dom-
> ination of dollars! There is no America. There is no democracy.
> There is only IBM and ITT and AT&T and Dupont, Union
> Carbide and Exxon. Those are the nations of the world now.

The generals and commissars and dictators fight about
stretches of land and peasants' bodies for the right to hoist
their personal standards over republics with the trappings of
sovereignty but the status of undischarged bankrupts. In the
new Babel, electronic communications systems will squirt a
culturally homogenising mist over vast stretches of the globe
and its name shall be called Westernity. Little wonder that
grey-faced comrades in the Kremlin get frantic when they
hear Soviet young people whistling Beatles' tunes on the
streets of Moscow.

Who is the Enemy?
In the old world, before the electronic media changed most
things, diplomacy was based on concepts of Them and Us
which had to do with distance; the outsider was traditionally

cast as an enemy until he proved otherwise. But communications technology has done strange things to this sense of hostile space between human beings. The argument runs roughly as follows.

Ways of communicating affect not only social organisation and culture but also the structure of language. It is a truism that people think with and through language – there is actually a very pompous sounding name for this reasonably obvious insight, the Sapir-Whorf hypothesis. This states that the person who acquires a language gains not only a way of talking but a way of seeing, of organising experience. Language has built into its grammar and lexicon the very structure of perception.

Speech was the first of the mass media. It gave rise to oral cultures in which people believed more easily what they heard than what they saw. And since all cultures have to locate themselves in time and space, oral societies had a sense of continuity over time, but were spatially discontinuous. Things were reasonably harmonious between generations within the same society, but there were vast differences and often conflicts with other societies a hundred miles or so apart. Time bound oral cultures together, space separated them.

When oral cultures gave place first to print and then the electronic media such as radio, television and films, the relationship between time and space was reversed. A common time-sense was essential to oral societies because they had to remember, to carry knowledge in their heads – they could not write it down. Once the language changed from speech to print and then to the electronic image, perceptions changed as well – people located themselves differently within the dimensions of space and time. A sense of time was not so important because the new media could record and play back the past at will. It was space which became continuous because the airwaves could annihilate distance, overleaping natural barriers and political frontiers.

It would be naive to suggest that the abolition of distance has produced some kind of universal cultural humanoid. The principles of diversity seem to be built into the human species regardless of physical location, whether close to or distant from the rest of one's own kind. But it is time differences that now seem more difficult to bridge than spatial ones in the global village. In primitive societies, the gulf between generations was less pronounced than that between regions. In the new Babel, the gulf between generations assumes ever greater significance.

In time-bound societies, the old are venerated by the young as repositories of wisdom and tradition; in space-bound electronic societies where knowledge is expanding at an exponential rate, the old are more likely to be pitied than respected by the young because they are not abreast of the latest technological fad. The American teenager and his Russian counterpart seem to have more in common with each other by way of a world-view than they have with their respective parents.

The electronic media have forged links between societies once spatially distant and therefore considered hostile. But the price has been to open up gulfs between generations within Babel. In spite of the massive propaganda campaigns aimed to prove that the absolute enemy is on the other side of an Iron or Bamboo Curtain, the reality seems to be that an equally inveterate enemy is within the castle walls. The clash of world-views occurs not only in the General Assembly of the United Nations but round the family table.

The traditional purpose of religion, according to the derivation of the word, is to bind people together at the most fundamental level. The Pauline assertion that in Christ there is neither Jew nor Greek, male nor female, bond nor free, was made in a time-bound society in which the divisions were spatial. The gulf between generations may prove a most formidable challenge to Christian mission because the electronic media abolish space but open up time gulfs.

TEN

What about the Church?

Communications Models

A current jargon term is ecclesial cybernetics. Cybernetics is the study of the transmission of information for the purposes of communication and control in the large organisation. Curiously enough, St Paul would have had less trouble with the term than we may have. When in 1 Corinthians 12: 28, he extolled the 'power of governing' as a gift of the Spirit, the Greek word is cognate with *kubernetes* – a helmsman or pilot. So ecclesial cybernetics is about the problems of communication and control in the Church.

The term was coined by the US Catholic theologian, Patrick Granfield[35] and he has written a fascinating book on the subject. He offers a systems analysis of authority and decision-making in the Roman Catholic Church in terms of the way information is handled. His cybernetic definition of the Church is a little less lyrical than those found in the Bible and it will be some time before the most radical liturgical reviser gets round to using it, 'The Church is a nonlinear, multiple-loop-feedback system with variable elements.' Amen to that. Terms like input, output, feedback and entropy replace the familiar categories of theology; thus, the local church is a unit of negative entropy, dialogue is feedback, and Christ's struggle on the Cross was against the forces of entropy.

In particular, Granfield sees information feedback as the clue to the way the Church can accomplish the task set out in the tag, *Ecclesia semper reformanda* – the Church must ever be reformed. Feedback is the essential agency of internal change; it helps to clarify doctrine, makes leadership more responsive to the needs of those led and defines discipleship because it is through the input, output and feedback of its members that the Church remains 'relevant'.

Granfield's terminology and approach may be forbidding, but he is drawing attention to an important truth. Every aspect of the Church's life is affected by the way it handles information. It is, in short, a communications model which is acutely sensitive to the general communications environment around it. If there is congruence between the customary mode of communication in the Church and that outside it, an open system is set up – to use the jargon of cybernetics. The Church uses information dynamically to sustain, develop and reform itself and to affect the life of the community.

When the Church's communication model is antipathetic to that of the outside environment a closed system results in which there is little interaction between the two. The Church's life is static, its structures fossilised and its impact on society virtually that of a museum exhibit behind glass.

The contrast cannot be as stark as this, of course. The Church can never be hermetically sealed off from a world its members inhabit. They share the daily life of a number of systems, open and closed, centred on work, family, social pursuits and public interests. Far from the Church and the world being discrete spheres, the Church is that part of the world shot through with the reconciling power of God evinced in the lives of its members. What can happen, however, through religious obscurantism, is that Christians pigeon-hole information and keep data relevant to Church and world rigorously separate. They speak the language of Babel in the street and that of Zion in the pew.

So the communications style and technology of the Television Age has the same vital significance for the Church as the composition of the water has to a fish. The particular communications model of the Church must resonate with the communications environment around it. But has the Church any choice? Can it assume or discard communications models at will? Where in fact do they come from?

Well, we can start from this obvious point. In two senses, the Church is a mystery. Christians cannot objectify the Church, get an unbiased view of it, because their life is intertwined with it to a point beyond unravelling. Much more fundamentally, the Church is a mystery because it is imbued with the hidden presence of God, and this takes it out of any known category of social institution or secular organisation.

So the essence of the Church must be communicated to people in the way mysteries have been mediated since the dawn of human history – through images.

The word 'image' has a sinister ring; the proscriptions of the Second Commandment echo all round it. But there is that construct given wide theological currency by the late Bishop Ian Ramsay, of Durham – the model. Unlike the image which the credulous have sometimes believed had unearthly powers locked up in it, no-one confuses a model with the real thing. You can treat a model without undue respect, stretching it this way and that to see what deductions might be drawn from it.

But images or models cannot be applied to the Church at will; they must be rooted in the self-understanding of the faithful. Paul Minear, who lists over ninety images of the Church in the New Testament, puts it this way,

> The Church's inner cohesion, its esprit de corps, derive from a dominant image of itself, even though that image remains inarticulately imbedded in subconscious strata. If an un-authentic image dominates its consciousness, there will first be subtle signs of malaise, followed by more overt tokens of communal deterioration. If an authentic image is recognised at verbal level but denied in practice, there will also follow sure disintegration of the ligaments of corporate life.[36]

Christians begin to visualise themselves and organise their common life according to those images or models which are conceived through preaching, liturgy and religious education to communicate most aptly their experience of God. Each model has its own language and value system; it addresses certain problems vigorously but cannot cope with others. Whatever the model, because it is derived from finite experience it cannot adequately represent the mystery of divine grace. Still, models have practical value provided they are not treated as exclusive or comprehensive statements of truths they can only hint at.

Just as no man is an island, so no model is a monolith. Models must interpenetrate, augment and challenge each other. From the New Testament onwards, theological thinking about the Church has been so wide-ranging and rich that every attempt to put it into words runs the risk of logical incoherence and verbal confusion. Any worth-while model must reflect this spiritual prodigality without trying to fit a straitjacket upon it.

Avery Dulles, the American Jesuit, has analysed five such models of the Church.[37] He evaluates each according to such standards as its basis in Scripture and tradition, ability to offer Christians a corporate sense of identity and its success in portraying an up-to-date religious experience which links Christians to God, to one another and to society generally.

I would wish to add another test. What sort of communication is at work within a particular model and therefore how is it likely to perform in the Television Age? This theme is implicit in Dulles' exposition but is worth spelling out. Each model is, of course, a drastic over-simplification of complex Biblical and theological evidence in order to permit the drawing of sharp, impressionistic morals.

There is the *institutional* model of the Church. The emphasis is on structures of power dominated by the clergy. The ethos is that of a monarchy strictly governed by rules handed down from the top. There is much play upon statistics, buildings, endowments, prerogatives and prestige. The whole mood is triumphalist, with few concessions made to the spirit of the age. Membership is sharply defined and established on a quasi-legal basis – in a word, you are clearly in or out; there are no blurred edges at the frontiers of loyalty, no 'invisible' members or secret disciples.

Structurally, the symbolism is that of the sumptuous edifice enclosing sacred space exclusively dedicated to the worship of Almighty God. The Church is the supreme guardian of revelation in the sense of a body of doctrine handed down from the apostles who got it from the mouth of Christ. It is mediated to the people by a priestly hierarchy in the form of propositions through which clarity of definition is sought in order that truth and error might be sharply differentiated. It is an essentially one-way communications network where the laity are passive receivers. And at the boundary between the Church and the world is a high wall to keep out influences that might pollute the purity of the truth hoarded within.

The model of the Church as *herald* offers a power structure of a different kind. In this type, the Word is sovereign – incarnate in Christ, written in the Bible and proclaimed in the sermon. The Church is essentially an auditorium for the hearing of the Word. The preacher is prince and the congregation are the first fruits of the harvest of the Gospel and in turn become witnesses and heralds. This Gospel is not a series of propositional truths but an event realised through the speaking of the language of faith. These power-charged words call the community of faith into being and declare the presence of Christ with his people. Forms of Church government are not considered very important though the congregational pattern is common.

Structurally, the symbolism is austere, for as Karl Barth commented, 'The Reformers sternly took from us everything but the Bible.' The church building is an assembly place in which acoustics are more important than ornamentation; the pulpit dominates the communion table and towers above the faithful. Enthroned is no pope or bishop but the Word of God. It is an environment saturated with words – in preaching, praise, prayer and testimony. The spiritual kin of Luther rejoice in the marrying of those words to music; the kin of Calvin are not unanimously agreed that it is seemly so to do.

The kerygmatic model is an authoritarian communications network – the truth is proclaimed and the people hear it or 'sit under it' as the quaint phrase has it. Discussion about interpretation is only permitted within limits. In the more extreme versions, intelligence from the world barely impinges on the talk within the walls except to furnish the material of sermon illustration and occasions for prayer.

The *communion* model appears in three main guises which have varying Biblical warrant and practical differences – the Body of Christ, the People of God and the Fellowship of the Holy Spirit. These are basically Biblical metaphors given corporeal form to create not just sociological units but networks of grace. The union of members with one another and their common link with Christ is neither organic nor legalistic – it is mystical and devotional, primarily internal but expressed in external bonds of creeds, worship and gathered fellowship.

In this model, the Church is not just a vehicle for getting penitent sinners to heaven, it exists for its own sake. Once people are in the Church they are fulfilling the purpose of their existence to some extent – and whether they are in the Church or not, only Christ knows. This model is very hospitable to the concept of invisible membership. Indeed, so generous are the judgments often made by members about the state of grace of their fellow human beings outside the Church that it is hard to see what the point of evangelism is at all.

No special structures and symbolically rich furnishings are needed to house and order the life of these communities. It is enough that members are together, face to face, in Spirit-inspired fellowship. Private homes, public halls, the open air – all that is required is space, freedom from clutter, so that the people can act as the Spirit leads them. Formal liturgies are often thought to be as inhibiting as a detailed programme at a party.

These Christians claim to see the world through the eyes of Christ, and this is both liberating and challenging. Lack of doctrinal rigour, however, opens them to the temptation of endorsing one sort of humanism or another because there happens to be a lot of it around and it does more good than harm.

As a communications network, this model is so permeable by the general environment as to be open to all the confusions of information overload. On the one hand, all knowledge is affirmed as testifying to Christ who is the Truth, on the other, revelation is sought not in any body of truth but through mystical communion with God – which can become a self-justifying emotional experience.

The model of the Church as *servant* is the only one which gives the world priority over the Church. In other models, the world comes to God through the Church and God comes to the world through the Church. Here, it is the world and not the Church which is the House of God, the place where He is sought and worshipped. Since by definition a servant lives and works in someone else's house, the Church as servant does not seek to mark out any sacred ground; it follows Jesus who is the man for others wherever He leads but invariably to a prophetic ministry among the poor and underprivileged.

Structurally, the symbolism is of a strictly utilitarian building in harmony with its secular surroundings and capable of being put to all kinds of everyday uses. There is little emphasis placed upon Church membership or patterns of ecclesiastical government. In fact, it is the Kingdom not the Church which is the structure these Christians are concerned with – they seek to 'raise', 'build' or 'realise' it at the heart of society. The boundaries of the Church are potentially coextensive with those of the world itself. The vision is of one baptism, which is birth, and only one sacramental table at which every member of the human race will sit down by right and be fed.

In a sense, this is not a formal communications model at all since the Church is a stream of influence rather than a discrete structure – the appropriate image is more a swirl of colour in water than a rock. Concrete acts of discipleship say all that is necessary, and in contrast to the kerygmatic model, the Church like a good servant listens rather than speaks, allowing the world, as the saying goes, to set the agenda and often talk its way through the items as well.

The fifth model is that of the Church as *sacrament.* This model combines certain elements of both the institutional and communion models. The Church has a coherent structure yet it is filled not with legalistic truth nor dead tradition but with the abounding life of the Spirit. The rationale of this model is the assertion that Christ is God's sacrament because in Him divine grace has become tangible; but not only in Him, in all who are joined to Him in faith, hope and love.

Like all sacraments, the Church is grace made visible. And visibility implies some structure – the Church and not-the-Church must be clearly distinguishable. But because it is *grace* that is made visible, the emphasis is on a communion of love rather than a legally constituted body.

The highest priority is given to liturgy for this is the fountain from which the Church's power flows. The faithful are fused together with Christ and one another at the holy table, and also with those who, before them back to apostolic times, have made the same confession. Because the Church is a sacrament, the unity of Christian people must be visible, and so ecumenicism is enthusiastically endorsed. Nor does strong ecclesiastical identity produce by contrast a damning estimate of secular culture or other religious traditions. It is acknowledged that the grace of Christ has been given to all humanity and not just to the faithful.

As a communications model, the Church as sacrament can deploy the whole range of verbal, pictorial and dramatic symbolism because it is not so much trying to articulate a message as to be the message – in three dimensions, exploiting all the human senses.

It is obvious that none of these models on its own is remotely adequate to summarise the nature and work of any Christian congregation in the real world. Indeed, one congregation at various points in its history may, under different leadership, move in self-understanding between a number of the models. And at any given time, a congregation making a serious stab at Christian witness will find itself combining elements of all five.

For instance, the Church as sacrament, which seems to me to be the most fruitful model for the Television Age, needs to borrow structure from the institutional model because it must have a clear outline in order to be an effectual sign. But it also needs the insight about loving communion to identify the sign as pointing to Christ. And, without preaching, the bread of life is not broken. Finally, the acceptance of humble service dramatises the practical outworkings of the grace of Christ.

There can never be full resonance between a secular communications environment and any model of the Church, whether derived from Scripture or evolved by Christians to meet the needs of the moment. There is a strand in Christian revelation which does not tend towards greater clarity, wider understanding and universal accessibility. One of the less attractive of Christ's offices is that of sign of contradiction – 'He is destined to be a sign which men reject. Many in Israel will stand or fall because of him . . .' This is the harsh ground-bass counterpoint to the theme of Incarnation as divine communication. It is echoed in Christ's terse deflation of the earliest Christian communicators – 'Tell no man!'

Whatever the models invented to mediate it, the essence of the mystery which is the Church will always generate tension, ambiguity and conflict in any culture. And this tension cannot be resolved by letting go of either end of it. The current controversy over liturgical reform demonstrates the point. Some radical revisers seek an accommodation with secular culture that results in ritual language too fragile to bear the weight of mystery. The staunchest King James enthusiasts, on the other hand, seem to believe that mystery finally dissolved without remainder into the language of the sixteenth century and that the ritual incantation of words which are strictly without contemporary meaning convey power. In so-called primitive societies, this is called magic.

Throughout its history, Christianity has been embroiled in an endless war of myths. The Gospel challenges the myths

human beings perennially create to make sense of an
existence they fondly suppose to be free of God. The
Television Age is already engaged in creating such a mythology. The search is for models of the Church which
maintain the tension with secular culture that the presence
and power of mystery requires without losing all points
of contact. If one's doctrine of creation is audacious
enough, it is possible to link the language of Babel with
the language of Zion as dialects of the same mother-tongue –
doxology – utterance in praise of God.

Cathode Ray Communicants

There is one other potent model of the Church which is not
rooted in the Bible but is a product of the Television Age
itself – the so-called electronic church. At present, it is largely
an American phenomenon but there is the promise or threat
of its being exported to the United Kingdom once cable and
satellite channels are in place and anyone can buy time on
them.

Though a tremendous amount has been written and said
on the subject, myths abound about the role and influence of
the electronic church in American life, so a brief sketch is
necessary because it is a religious and social force of the
Television Age which cannot be ignored.

The term 'electric church' was invented in the 1970s by the
evangelist Ben Armstrong, who wrote, 'In this vision, I saw
the electric church as a revolutionary form of the worshipping, witnessing Church that existed twenty centuries
ago... as in New Testament times, so in the electronic
church worship once again takes place in the home.'[38] Many
of the best-known television evangelists resist the term
however and insist that they are not in the business of
creating a substitute or para-church. Their desire is to direct
converts into the mainline Churches.

The mainline Churches beg to differ. They charge that the
electronic evangelists began by driving them out of
television through being prepared to buy the time which was
once offered to the Churches free. In 1960 when the Federal
Communications Commission ruled that television stations

could discharge their public service obligations by accepting payment from religious bodies, most stations lost any inclination to give away valuable air time to the mainline Churches.

Having lost their television outlets, the mainline Churches then found there was a seepage of 'bodies and bucks' away from the pews and collection plates. There is little statistical evidence to back the claim that mainline Church membership has been swollen by the activities of the television evangelists. Most denominations are in a state of slow decline and the electronic church offers one convenient scapegoat – though the evidence is equivocal.

It is impossible to offer many generalisations about a group of religious television superstars as individualistic as Billy Graham, Oral Roberts, Rex Humbard, Jerry Falwell, Robert Schuller, Pat Robertson and Jimmy Swaggart. With the exception of Schuller, who is an exponent of Norman Vincent Peale's self-improvement Gospel, they are all conservative evangelicals or downright literalists. And whether or not they have evolved substitute Churches they have certainly created real industries.

In 1980, the top four television evangelists took a quarter of a billion dollars from the American public; the next five got a hundred million dollars between them. That is big business and represents not just television programmes but a huge retailing operation in tapes, cassettes, books, records, lapel badges, T-shirts and crosses.

If television made their work possible, computers have rendered it profitable. Word processors spew out millions of personally addressed letters; computers file and regurgitate endless data as part of an immensely professional and highly complex marketing operation. Converts have to be converted into contributors, enquirers must be recruited as customers. In an ever-widening but vicious circle, more and more financial supporters have to be won to pay for television time that gets ever more expensive in order to reach more and more viewers who will become financial supporters . . .

The evangelists' image on television screens may be

ephemeral but their organisations are solid enough as are the
institutions they have established to give themselves some
degree of immortality. Oral Roberts University, Jerry
Falwell's Liberty Baptist College, Pat Robertson's CBN
University and Jim Bakker's Heritage School of Evangelism
and Communication are, in different styles, splendid edifices
packed with the latest technology and busily engaged in
training the second generation of devotees. As these protégés
spread throughout the United States, critics claim to see the
ghostly outlines of mini-denominations emerging, though
no major evangelist will acknowledge such an intention.

Whatever may be thought of the content of their
programmes, it is beyond argument that the major television
evangelists are masters of the medium, obeying the first rule
of television – to provide good entertainment. Their
programmes are slick, technically excellent, and in professional standards of performance by musicians, actors,
dancers and so on, comparable to the best of the rest of
television output.

They have also mastered the forms and conventions of the
medium. While some evangelists like Billy Graham confine
themselves to preaching rallies, others go in for chat shows,
soap operas, cartoons, drama and studio panel games with
suitable prizes such as package tours of the Holy Land and
luxuriously-bound copies of the Bible.

Any identikit compilation of the Gospel they preach is
bound to be unfair to some evangelists and over-generous to
others. They offer simple solutions to complex problems –
personal conversion is the key, deliverance from any human
affliction from cancer to poverty the consequence. Their
enemies are communists, homosexuals and secular humanists – the last infest the media, Federal Government, schools
that teach evolution and the Supreme Court.

The goal of most television evangelists is not just to save
sinners but America itself; to call the Republic back to the
values and life-style of a day when every family said its
prayers, read the Bible, defended its property with a
Winchester rifle if necessary and enjoyed law and order
backed by the noose or electric chair. These themes hit home

at a time when conventional authority is in disarray and moral standards are clouded in ambiguity – at least to those who remember and romanticise the good old days.

There is a sense in which the electronic evangelists have been the inspiration of a counter-culture of the Right in the 'seventies and 'eighties to redress the balance of the 'sixties counter-culture of the Left with its drugs and drop-outs, Jesus freaks and flower-power, Vietnam protest and rejection of patriotism. These evangelists are politically conservative by conviction, because their reading of the Bible induces them to be and because their supporters are. *And* because too many of the mainline Churches in their view, are apostate – with their support for the World Council of Churches, their tolerance of liberal or radical theologies and enthusiasm for dialogue with Roman Catholics and humanists.

It was in the 1980 presidential election campaign that the electronic evangelists discovered their latent political power. Individual evangelists such as Billy Graham had been spiritual counsellors and prayer-partners of Presidents Eisenhower, Nixon, Ford and Carter, but there is no evidence that Dr Graham had attempted to shape government policy. He bolstered it, perhaps, as in his backing of the Vietnam War, but that was the extent of his political interventionism.

The New Christian Right, however, was an unashamedly political pressure group created in 1980 to ensure the election of a right-wing president and a right-wing congress to bring America back to God. And television evangelists, especially Jerry Falwell, leader of the Moral Majority, were the prophets, theologians and presiding geniuses of the movement. The very iconoclasts who had called down the wrath of God on the mainline Churches for deserting the Gospel and getting involved in politics now performed a complicated Biblical manoeuvre which enabled them to describe their own machinations as the tactics of Apocalypse. When Anti-Christ appears in the land, he must be fought with whatever weapons come to hand.

There were four reasons why the electronic evangelists

found themselves in a strategic political position in 1980. They were past masters at diagnosing America's ills in evocative, moralistic terms; their spiritual enemies invariably adopted left-wing political stances; every social movement of the Television Age lives or dies by its command of the mass media and the electronic evangelists are television practitioners of vast experience; and they alone knew exactly who the moral majority were – they had their names and address in millions on their computer print-outs.

The electronic evangelists have begun to export their Gospel to Latin America, the Far East and Africa. Hundreds of television stations in the so-called developing world now transmit their programmes. Few doubt their enthusiasm to share in the great commission of Matthew 28 – to preach the Gospel to all nations – but the harsher critics claim to see two additional motives in this electronic outreach. Their militant anti-communism accords well with the United States' ideological struggle to prevent the Third World going Red. And the plain truth is that they have saturated the domestic market and now, like all forms of capitalist enterprise, need to seek new sources of funds beyond the shores of the United States.

One crucial question remains: who actually watches the programmes of the electronic evangelists? In a painstaking piece of research, Peter Horsefield[39] has offered some answers and cut through the fog generated by the over-blown claims of supporters and deflationary estimates of the critics. He took the period 1950/80 and some of his conclusions are as follows:

- 24% of the adult population of America watch at least one hour's religious television every week.
- twice as many women as men watch the programmes and roughly two-thirds of viewers are over 50 years of age.
- proportionately, fewer people in the higher social and educational brackets watch the electronic evangelists; and comparatively few adolescents are attracted.
- 18% of those who do watch claim some religious allegiance.
- viewing is high in Protestant fundamentalist groups and highest amongst those who claim some conversion experience.

- 28% of the unchurched polled in 1978 claimed to have watched one or more of the programmes in the previous month – this figure included TV addicts who habitually leave their sets on all day and much of the night.
- the audience for these programmes apparently peaked in 1977 and is now stable or fractionally in decline. The appeal directors of several of the evangelical organisations contend that the market is now saturated.

It would be foolish on the basis of such statistical evidence to start writing the obituary notice of the electronic church. These television evangelists are merely one highly visible and vocal element in a much more complex religious and cultural phenomenon in the United States. Jeremy Rifkin, a perceptive observer of the US religious scene, sums up the situation this way:

> The evangelical community is amassing a base of potential power that dwarfs every other competing interest in American society. A close look at the evangelical communications network ... should convince even the sceptic that it is now the single most important cultural force in American life ...

It would be a mistake to judge the electronic church solely in terms of its political and cultural significance. Through it people are led to faith. Electronic evangelists invade people's homes bringing with them a vivid and exuberant spirituality and sheer good company. They also remind viewers of the religious option when life is getting them down. Their vigour challenges Churches grown torpid and political movements become leaden and boring. And Christians have much to learn from their virtuosity in applying technology to religious communication.

The American way of life as depicted by the electronic evangelists is circumscribed and in some particulars downright wrong, but it is a picture of the world with which people can identify – and who else is offering one? And yet ... emotional reassurance is not enough. A gospel evacuated of theological rigour and ethical commitment is both crippled and crippling.

Possibly the greatest count against most of the electronic

evangelists is that they are trying to foist on society a private, invisible church which the New Testament will not allow. Though their love for Jesus is sincere and fervent, it is hard to resist the conclusion that they are actually trying to put the Incarnation into reverse by etherialising the Word.

Thus, I make my weekly appearance at the electronic church, or rather, it makes its weekly appearance before me. I always get my favourite seat, I don't need a Sunday suit and I'll have no problem parking my car or waiting for public transport. The whole thing need cost me little more than the energy it takes to switch on the set and that required to post off a cheque afterwards if I feel like it.

The electronic evangelist concentrates massively on my favourite subject – me; my problems, my wealth, health and happiness. If he makes me feel a miserable sinner at the outset of his sermon I'll be restored to bonhomie by the end because he'll assure me just how easy it is to be saved.

Other human beings need not impinge on my conscious-ness at all except collectively and in the form of an abstraction – sinners. Even those toe-stubbing stumbling blocks of the Gospel – the poor, old and outcast – are no problem. I see some of them there in the brightly-lit Cathedral of the Air, beaming away, the poor well-scrubbed, the old content and the outcasts happy and tensionless.

I secretly like the fact I don't have to rub shoulders with my fellow Christians who in real life I find cussed, hypercritical and unreasonable in their demands, spoken and unspoken, upon me. No need for silly arguments with the caretaker about the temperature of the sanctuary, with the organist about unfamiliar hymn tunes and with the minister about his unorthodox preaching. I know exactly what I am in for at the electronic church. It will be a nostalgic, reassuring experience, unblemished by coughs and splutters, restless children, dropped hymn books and creaking doors.

If communication is about self-disclosure then I am communing with an electronically induced spectre, and if I accept his invitation to write, I shall have dialogue with a word processor. If my birthday or the anniversary of a loved one's death is recalled by a suitable paragraph in the reply I get, it will be because a computer forgets nothing. Love given and reciprocated takes the form of an exchange of cheques and receipts. The costs of fellowship do not bear equally upon the spectral preacher and myself. I offer only a few dollars; he has to find millions. After all, he has to buy the computer.

That, of course, is certainly a parody; it could also be a warning.

The Clash of Symbols

Any religious experience capable of being passed on to others must be expressed in symbols. But once it is imprisoned in some language – whether of words, images or gestures – it loses its raw purity and inherits a history and location. Every language has evolved over time and emerged from some social setting that has determined its structure.

The body of spiritual truth contained in the Koran has inevitably been shaped by the style of the Arabic language and the region from which it came. Had Jesus been born in Africa rather than the Near East, the Gospel would have been different not only in style but also in structure because Bantu and Semitic languages encapsulate radically divergent notions of time and matter. Presumably God took this into account when choosing the Jews.

This means that, on the one hand, what fundamentalists call 'literal interpretation' is impossible because the language which conveys the truth is *human* language – it is the product of a long history and carries as cargo the impress of all kinds of experiences, many of which have nothing to do with religion. On the other hand, religious experience cannot be explained away as the mere reflection of a particular history and language structure. Peter Berger writes: 'Religion can be understood as a human projection because it is communicated in human symbols. But this very communication is motivated by an experience in which metahuman reality is injected into human life.[40]

As we have seen earlier, when traditional religious symbols lose their power, the human spirit seeks others through which to express itself because human beings are meaning-seeking creatures. And television is conveniently to hand as a most potent source of symbolism which is universally accessible, intellectually undemanding and warmly evocative. So the scene is set for a clash of symbols because Christianity, though embattled, is still a symbol system of great significance in our society.

But the balance of power has shifted. In medieval times, Christianity was the giant on to whose territory rivals trespassed at their peril. Her symbols dominated; her stories were the official accounts of experience. Now Christianity operates within a secular order over which the aerial rather than the Cross towers as an effectual symbol.

When either symbol system enters the heartland of the other, strange things happen. We have already looked at the ambiguities of television worship; they result in part from trying to project experiences habitually couched in one language system through the prism of another. What of the impact of television myth and symbolism on the Church's domestic life?

Most Christians are aware that the clash of symbolism which reverberates throughout their daily lives also echoes round the sanctuary. Not even the thickest church or chapel wall can resist the shock waves of the information explosion. Quite simply, Christians know more, and they know it sooner. They have a sober appreciation of the dimensions and densities of the world, and its tragedies and inanities impinge on their consciousness almost as soon as they occur.

Television alone cannot take the credit for this. Ease and cheapness of travel, mass education and the power of the other public media all have their effect. But for intensity of impact, visual intelligence instantaneously transmitted is unrivalled. The result is to demythologise much of the Church's traditional rhetoric.

When John Wesley proclaimed the whole world to be his parish, his listeners could have had no conception, except by way of flights of imagination or hearsay, what the magnitude of that evangelical and pastoral task was. His affirmation still has meaning as a metaphor – 'I intend to claim all that the Bible means by "world" for Christ.' As a summons to global mission in the geographical sense, which is how his immediate followers interpreted it, Wesley's challenge must reckon with a daunting view of the world available to modern Christians by way of the small screen – endless ranks of uniformed Chinese extolling Mao, Asia's teeming millions pouring in and out of temples, devout Muslims all over the world turning east to pray for the prescribed number of times a day.

The shrill tones of evangelical triumphalism fashionable a generation or so ago are now muffled with judicious talk about dialogue, mutual understanding and the congruence of many-sided truth. The ordinary Christian, nurtured on a diet of hymnody, missionary rhetoric and Sunday-school lessons confidently predicting the whole world won for Christ sooner or later, finds the clash of symbolism unnerving. The world as viewed through the window of the small screen shows little evidence of advancing Christian imperialism. Great religions such as Hinduism, Islam, Buddhism and Taoism seem to fit their cultural mould snugly and express aptly the spiritual genius of their devotees.

Television has vastly speeded the process of demythologising the great religions of the world. Before Britain became a visibly multi-faith society, the average Christian found out about, say, Hinduism, either through his reading or from the accounts given by returned travellers, especially missionaries – some of whom had a highly sensitive appreciation of another faith but were hardly disinterested witnesses.

Hundreds of millions of people were lumped together as the targets of Christian mission. Their God-given humanity was usually given proper respect, but their spirituality was judged on the basis of sketchy knowledge of customs and practices mostly shrouded in mystery. The Second World War – which set millions of people on the move between continents – cheap air travel and, pre-eminently, television changed all that. Television cameras traversed seven continents recording the cultural and artistic richness of non-Western peoples and hinting at the immense spiritual vitality in their religions.

The thing which strikes the armchair traveller above all else is the seeming inevitability of the great religions, their essential rightness within a given cultural context. That, of course, is a highly partial view, too. I claimed that television demythologised the great religions. More accurately, it has remythologised them. They are treated as part of the main flow of a broad naturalistic view of the planet, its wild life, scenic vistas, exotic architecture and richly diverse human types. The camera has both rationalised and romanticised the life of the temple, mosque and shrine.

So Christians in the pew find themselves at the impact point of a clash of symbolism, trying to reconcile television's highly stylised version of the world's religions with the response offered by various theologies of mission, also highly stylised.

I need not labour the point. Not only the Church's understanding of mission but most aspects of its life suffer the impact of this clash of symbols offering different explanations of the same reality. It's a perennial problem for preachers required to mine the raw material of sermons from whatever vein of experience preoccupies the congregation. For years they have had to take account of the televisually mediated account of the world.

Most preachers use television as the source of parable. Because people in the street, at work, or on public transport discuss them, television programmes are significant, however trivial their content, since human lives touch each other through them. The kind of community formed by gossip about 'Match of the Day' or 'Coronation Street' may be superficial and ephemeral, but it is one more ring main through which the pulses of the Gospel might surge.

Much of the sermon in the classical era of preaching was taken up with spellbinding narrative and graphic verbal pictures. Now what counts is the ability to test whether the spirits, as expressed in secular imagery, are of God. Neither oratory nor learning is as essential to this task as spiritual perception. There was a time when the preacher might be the cleverest person the average congregation had heard. Now TV gurus of great articularity and much knowledge parade before them on the small screen every night. Wisdom is a rarer commodity.

The modern sermon is a product of literary culture capable of flourishing in the Television Age because it is a ritual act as structured as an intricate dance step and shaped to take its due place in the flow of liturgy. But even here television has its impact – not only on the preacher's repertoire of imagery but also on the congregation's attention span.

The electronic media have tutored a whole generation to get the point of information quickly, so the attention span has contracted. The thirty-second commercial, the three-minute news report, the ten-minute variety act – these make limited claims on the viewer's attention, whereas previous generations were attuned to the forty-five-minute lecture, the fifty-minute classroom lesson and the thirty-minute sermon. Though the faithful love the exquisitely slow build-up to a totally predictable conclusion, those outside the charmed circle find the sermon a very laboured way of communicating information.

In the clash of symbolisms, Protestantism is peculiarly vulnerable to the assaults of television's rich imagery because of that endemic disease – excess verbalisation, wordiness beyond belief. Cataracts of words, prayed, preached and sung, characterise a fervent but monotone spiritual experience in which the fire in the believer's soul seems all too often to turn to ashes on his lips. Language isolated from its non-verbal resonances skitters along the surface of life, filling the mind with matters of fact and excluding matters of myth. It creates a religious subculture of compulsive explainers and expounders.

The warmed heart and evangelical experience are treasured in Protestantism, but they are too often wrapped up in words and subjected to deft interpretation which squeezes the mystery out of them. This is how the Church is reduced to a structure of the intellect. Experience is filtered through a verbal grid and realities which cannot be spoken of are treated with scepticism if not downright suspicion. It was verbal exhaustion that drove Albert Schweitzer out to

Lambarene as a missionary doctor because, he said, he wanted to do good without having to say anything.

But Christianity is not only a structure of the intellect, it is also a structure of experience through which *felt* knowledge that eludes any dragooning by words fires the imagination and generates visionary energy. It is what happened to St Thomas Aquinas when he laid aside his monumental literary edifice in the face of a wordless vision. He wrote, 'All that I have written seems to me like straw compared with what has now been revealed to me.' Symbols of transcendence work this miracle and words alone cannot carry them.

So the Protestantism of the orderly mind, calloused vocal chords, under-used eyesight and withered imagination is ill-equipped to confront the rich visual imagery of television. For television is a structure of experience too, through which a view of reality which engages the imagination can be instantaneously absorbed without being verbalised. It may be a poor substitute for the real thing, but the starving imagination like the empty belly is remarkably catholic in its tastes.

The clash of symbolism *within* the Church may be discomfiting but the importance *of* the Church as a symbol in the Television Age will grow. McLuhan may rhapsodise the global village created by television but it is the fake community of a honeycomb of hermits' cells in a cliff wall. The Church is a public symbol that challenges the privatisation of life; a symbol of assembly which works against isolation and fragmentation; a symbol of corporate action at a time of individual passivity.

In Old Testament times, the word *ecclesia* meant just that – an assembly of the people, for politics, for war, for entertainment. We have sacralised it to the point where the ecclesiastical refers simply to the domestic economy of the Church. The term needs to be reclaimed for its original Biblical meaning. The Church's role in facilitating face-to-face encounter between whole people, who touch and sing and tell stories and do things together, is its true ecclesial purpose.

A resurgence of image-making ought not to be beyond a

Church whose Lord mediated himself through a multitude of things that captivated the senses – bread, water, sweat, silver, gold, a couple of crossed lines, blood, white, a cry, lover, fish, vinegar, purple.[41]

This mediation of the transcendent through the finite, the specific, the concrete, will be part of the Church's constant war in the Television Age against abstractions, impossible expectations and romantic dreaming – in a word, the old gnosticism which has been driven out into the desert often throughout Christian history, but always creeps back, like the demoniac, to flit among the tombs.

Television offers those who are so disposed a flight from the definite, the concrete, the hard-edged into a two-dimensional realm where, as in a dream, the spirit soars free; and, as in a dream, the link with reality is tenuous and jumbled. It provides ghostly company to people who shrink from real encounter; and for those who recoil from the scandal of the Cross, it projects a pantheon of glowing gods and goddesses unblemished by nailmarks in their hands.

The old gnostics hated the admixture of the holy and the human. They wanted truth without struggle, energy without sweat, personality unmarked by evidence of mortality. The new gnostics can deliver such unearthly perfection. Television celebrities stream across the screen, immaculate, gleaming with health and throbbing with happiness. Every vestige of human weakness is banished by a benign conspiracy of make-up girls, wardrobe staff, lighting experts and tactful camera directors.

Television must not be written off because it is the unwitting agent which breathed new life into an old heresy. There is much about it that is good and wholesome and enjoyable. We must be clear just who is doing what to whom. Television can neither bless nor curse us without our connivance or indolence. When, in the early morning of Creation, God gave human beings dominion over the earth, he effectively countered in advance excuses such as Eve's, 'The serpent made me do it,' or Adam's 'Technology is beyond me; we'll just have to hope for the best!'

Nevertheless, because human beings are incurably religious, they will invest anything that has secular potency with sacred meaning if no other gods are conveniently to hand. What is wrong with the human desire to escape the circumscribing realities of a tough existence, to fantasise a little, to hope a particle or two of star-dust might touch one's shoulder, to press one's nose against the window of the television screen and enjoy vicariously the radiant life of the golden people? Nothing – except this: the totality of experiences such as these eventually form the gnostic mind.

The sacramental and liturgical life of the Church is an attack on the gnostic mind. Christianity is about flesh lacerated and blood spilt, about the weight of hands laid upon us and water stinging the skin or taking away our breath as we plunge under the healing stream. The liturgical rites nail down particulars and challenge expansive generalities.

The marriage service strikes at the jugular of romantic love with hard talk about duty, duration and loyalty beyond the call of inclination. Even that apparently outmoded institution, the Christian Sabbath, becomes a potent symbol of human liberation – proclaiming freedom from the domination of the lords of space and time who, throughout the week, impose on us the rituals of habitual labour at set hours in temples hallowed for productive purposes.

The Church exists to ensure that the human being's sacramental consciousness does not atrophy in an age of appearances where images float through the ether and voices call out from the empty air. The raison d'être of the Church is to bring the citizens of the Television Age into some relationship with a particular Jew who lived in a particular time and patrolled a particular space. Such pin-point accuracy spells the death of gnosticism.

St Augustine said the essence of idolatry is that mankind is tyrannised by the works of his own hands. The Church as sacrament proclaims the fact that technology cut off from any transcendent reference is strictly meaningless. Bread is just baked flour unless it is blessed and broken. Television is just a device unless through its distortions the self can reach out for some kind of enduring purpose, some undying meaning. And who is going to go on nagging about such awkward but persistent truths if not the Church?

ELEVEN

Christianity as Communication

Why ought the Church to take more than a passing, intelligent interest in the question of changes in communications technology – except as a potential customer always willing to give the latest gadgetry a try in transmitting the old, old story? Christians who believe the Holy Spirit will make plain a Gospel couched in language not universally accessible in our day wonder why there should be such fuss about television. For them, it is just the latest of those 'little systems' which according to Tennyson,

> Have their day and cease to be
> For Thou, O Lord, art more than they!

An indubitable if somewhat chilly truth.

There is, however, another view. Radical changes in communications technology are not simply of interest to the Church, but profoundly affect its structure because the Church *is* a communications system. A highly impressionistic but not wholly inaccurate account of Church history can be given by correlating changes in the Church's life and witness with the evolution of mass media.

For instance, the manuscript era which followed the age of the apostles created the literate clerk or clergyman and made university theologians in the high Middle Ages the power behind papal and episcopal thrones.[42] The illiterate masses listened respectfully to the scholars but fed their souls on a rich variety of non-verbal media – liturgical action, ecclesiastical architecture, statuary, painting, stained glass and mystery plays.

The age of print made it possible to put a Bible in anybody's hands, established the Reformation, accelerated literacy, inspired religious individualism and allowed Luther to appeal to the Bible against the Pope and bishops. Print made easier the exact and mass reproduction of complex ideas, authoritative texts and abstract definitions – all the grand tradition of theology, in fact.

Such broad sweeps of history may take only a few sentences to describe or at least caricature, but they require hundreds of years to work themselves through. Since the Age of Television has barely dawned, it is foolhardy and premature to draw conclusions about the likely impact of the electronic media on the Church. Before essaying a few intelligent guesses, I want to examine the notion of Christianity as a communications system.

The Talkative God

Imagine a God who has no interest in making contact with his creation, who sits tight-lipped in heaven like Rodin's *Thinker,* brooding about whatever preoccupies the mind of a lonely deity. Then consider human creatures who have no capacity or appetite for reaching out towards the one who has made them and keeps them in being, who are hopelessly earthbound even in their thoughts and imagination. Either eventuality would make Christianity impossible or at least render it superfluous. For Christianity is a summary of all the ways that God and His creation can be in touch.

Christianity may be described as a faith, a religion or a way of life. It could equally well be called a system of communication and shares an open secret with its elder brother Judaism and its younger cousin Islam – that God is talkative by nature. He is given to gracious acts of self-disclosure.

Self-disclosure is the master-concept of communication which distinguishes it from raw information. Information is the passing-on of bits of intelligence; communication is about the self-disclosure of the communicator in the act of passing on bits of intelligence – hence, George Gerbner's well-known definition of communication, 'social interaction regulated by messages'.

The heart of Christianity is the communication of divine life to human beings through the incarnate life of Jesus Christ. Traditionally, the Church has understood Christ to be the communicated self-expression of God. In a twist which anticipated Marshall McLuhan by a couple of thousand years, Jesus is declared to be both medium and message – His person and work are inextricable. To 'preach Christ' or to 'preach the Gospel' or to 'preach salvation' is not to discourse about three separate things but to highlight the identity of medium and message from three different angles.

Theologians who are taken with the notion of Christianity as a system of communication usually hold one of two views. Some claim that the ultimate aim of *all* communication is to reveal God in our midst because human beings are made in His image and have a deep urge to share with others in God's self-communication. The other view is that the divine process of self-communication is a model of what all true communication between human beings should be like.

Either way, the central doctrines of Christianity are interpreted as models of communication, starting with the Trinity. There is appeal to New Testament passages which speak of the intimate communication that exists between the persons of the Godhead expressed in dynamic love. The orthodox believer might marshal the texts as follows: the Father speaks of, 'My beloved Son in whom I am well pleased'. The incarnate Son said, 'I came forth from the Father and have come into the world. Again I leave the world and go to the Father.' And of the Holy Spirit, Jesus said, 'When He, the Spirit of truth has come, He will guide you into all truth; for He will not speak on His own authority, but whatever He hears He will speak.'

On the other hand, Johannes Heinrichs, a theologically-trained communications specialist, puts it like this:

> Using the language of communication theory, we may say that in the Holy Spirit, the communicative exchange between the Father and Son is stabilised into a metacommunicative unity

which in turn is also not an abstract norm but personal life. The profound significance of the doctrine of the Trinity can provide endless food for meditation, particularly in the framework of communication theory.[43]

Yes, well ... one must allow each trade its jargon, but the point is made. Whether phrased in the comfortable words of scripture or in the argot of communications theory, the Trinitarian model is offered as the norm of true communication. Robert Webber, an American theologian, writes:

> Since communication within the Godhead is personal and relational, we may conclude the same is true of all meaningful communication. The Father, the Son and the Holy Spirit do not communicate with each other as if each were 'outside' or alienated from the other. The witness of triune communication is that it is always expressed through love. Love is the basis of good relations and, therefore, the context in which all good communication should take place. Certainly, trinitarian communication stands in judgment on our attempts to communicate in our impersonal and non-relational ways. It sets up a standard for communication ...[44]

Webber goes on to argue that the whole Christian scheme can be based on the image of God's communication with His creation which was disrupted by the fall of man and restored through the Incarnation. He deals at length with the Incarnation as the focal point of God's communication with human beings and seeks to show how it exactly meets the requirements of good communications as set out by the media experts, especially William Schramm whose rules are quoted as follows:

1. The message must be so designed and delivered as to gain the attention of the intended receiver.
2. The message must employ signs that refer to experience common to both sender and receiver.
3. The message must arouse personality needs in the receiver and suggest ways to meet those needs.
4. The message must suggest a way to meet those needs that is

appropriate to the group situation in which the receiver finds himself.[45]

Using a certain degree of homiletical cunning, Webber has little difficulty in matching up the Incarnation to Schramm's four points as an attention-getting, experience-sharing, need-arousing and need-answering communications model.

We do not need to appeal to technical communications theory for confirmation that Christian doctrines answer the problems of true communication – our everyday experience of the Christian life has taught us as much. We have learned that true communication can take place only between equals, therefore divine-human dialogue requires the Incarnation. As Calvin put it, 'God bends down, and lowering himself, lisps that we might hear and understand.'

We have discovered that in a fallen world the process of communication is distorted by such things as our desire for domination or hope of reward. The only words which escape this corruption are those that form part of the truth spoken in love. Even then there are dangers. To communicate with utter openness, to be reckless in self-disclosure, is to put oneself at someone else's mercy and risk the Cross.

A system of communication rather than a sporadic series of messages passing hither and thither requires a network or grid with some degree of permanence. The Christian grid is called the fellowship of the Holy Spirit – within which the gap between the communicating parties, in holiness if not distance, is bridged, in John Taylor's phrase, by the go-between God. The Spirit powers the system; there is an interchange of energy as well as information.

And when that gap between the parties is not just bridged but abolished, then communication solidifies into community – the new creation, the Kingdom of Heaven where members are united not only in meaning but in life.

Such perceptions are available to ordinary Christians innocent of expertise in formal communications theory, but it is a wholesome thing that increasing numbers of theologians are giving serious attention to this comparatively new discipline. In particular, Robert Webber and his patron James F. Engel are two scholars who are weaving together a conservative theology and an understanding of communications theory for the purposes of evangelism.

Their dogmatic assertiveness may jar on those who do not share this theological position. Stridency does erode to some extent the value of their insights about television, because electronic media transform rhetoric into shrillness and make ringing assertions sound like peremptory scolding. Still, given the magnitude of the challenge, all allies are welcome, and clear confidence in the Gospel is to be prized in a religiously ambiguous age.

Theology OF or Theology AND?

One of the best-known advocates of Christianity as a communication concept is Heinrich Kraemer, who set out his ideas in a book called *The Communication of the Christian Faith*. For him, communication is the fundamental divine fact, the essence of the nature of Christ and the basis for all human interaction. This position has not gone unchallenged. Some theologians are sceptical of basing a whole theology on a key-concept as abstract and ill-defined as communication. These critics weary of the proliferating sub-species of theology, especially those which are theologies-*of*... theology *of* communication, theology *of* liberation, theology *of* industry, and so on.

The opponents of the notion of a theology of communication insist that the rise of the electronic media does not justify a new branch of theology – old problems are just being thrown up in new guises and with greater urgency. There already exists a form of theology with the jaw-breaking name of hermeneutics whose task is to discover the meaning for our time of texts and messages which originated in a different age and culture.

There is a rather obvious problem about using, say, the Trinity as a model for communication – its basic structure cannot be reproduced in human life. The persons of the Trinity may be in a state of perfect communication, but it is communication without the aid of any media whatsoever.

How does this model help the poor benighted Christian communicator who is utterly dependent on the media?

Cess Hamelink, after a rigorous critical analysis of the theology of communication, writes:

> It is my conclusion that any 'theology of communication' which is primarily a theological approach to public communication, will offer a conceptual framework which is bound to apply inadequate definitions of structures and processes of public communication and consequently is not meaningful.[46]

Hamelink believes that the whole exercise of evolving a theology of communication is doomed because it takes place in a vacuum – any conclusions are reached deductively by analysing the terms 'theology' and 'communication'. It's all very airy fairy and unearthed in the social and political setting within which real communication must take place.

Even if a 'not proven' verdict is returned about the need for a theology of communication, the argument is valuable because it forces into prominence neglected issues to do with the medium of revelation rather than its message. Meanwhile most scholars interested in the subject seem to prefer the conjunctional to the genitive – theology *and* communication rather than the theology *of* communication. They are tackling the task in a piecemeal fashion by examining elements of religious communication in the light of their academic specialisms.[47]

The word-merchants concentrate on religious language. They study both the forms of language such as grammar and syntax and its content – narrative, parable, metaphor, symbol and myth. Does the sacred disappear when we no longer have the language which enables us to speak about it? If the old religious symbols no longer 'work', how may we replace them? If it is true, as Suzanne Langer claims, that the line between man and beast is the language line, what is there in the structure of language that points to our origins and destiny in God?

Then there are the aesthetes who look at human expression as set out in the whole field of arts from architecture and icon to contemporary forms such as films, drama, television and painting. What is the relationship between beauty and holiness? Does the truth we see suffer less distortion than the truth we hear or is it the role of Christian art to complement Christian discourse like words set to music? It may be that revelation through art obviates the need for developed arguments in propositional form, but how then do we construct any theory of religious self-understanding based on art without using the language of argument and discourse?

The culture-vultures follow McLuhan in approach if not in conclusions, and study the impact of the media on human culture. Using historical or psychological models, they plot shifting patterns of human consciousness against the changing forms of communication. Those who take this approach tend to polarise into happy optimists or despairing pessimists. The electronic media either offer exciting new possibilities for religious communication or else isolate people, privatise human life and choke us with floods of redundant information.

There are the theological mechanics who draw heavily on information theory and construct complex diagrams setting out variations of the sender-message-receiver analogue. Messages are encoded and decoded and dispatched in 'envelopes'. Those who are led to reflect on the theology of communication by way of experience in broadcasting tend to favour these Meccano-like models.

Dialogue is the key constituent of religious communication for Christians who harbour grave suspicions of the mass media and take Christ's example of face-to-face encounter as their pattern. They argue that God's revelation is aimed at setting up a dialogue with human beings which is like the discourse of friends and lovers. Small groups rather than mass audiences are the setting for true dialogue. This is the communications image favoured by those who write about the devotional life and the specialists in prayer who believe that communion with God ought to be the main pre-occupation of Christian communicators; all else, including an intelligible word to the world, will then be added as a bonus.

It is clear that what is loosely described as the theology of communication covers a vast area of human enquiry and the work being done in it is fragmented. Not only do academic specialisms isolate researchers, so also do geographical considerations. The North Americans are concerned to the point of obsession with the electronic church which is the most visible form of religious communication in vogue and also prompts angry theological and ethical questioning. The Europeans are massively philosophical and the British firmly Biblical in their approach to communication. Latin Americans and Africans worry about the cultural oppression which results from the export of the first world's communications technology; more positively, they concentrate on the smaller and older media.

The interest groups also have their angles. Professional broadcasters have added less than their fair share to the corpus of theological thinking about communication. They are so busy making programmes they have little leisure to reflect on the significance of what they are doing. Theorists, on the other hand, are often so innocent of the technical, managerial and economic realities of broadcasting that their work seems anchored in mid-air. Local church groups react positively to the mass media by asking the how-can-we-use-them questions, and negatively by damning them for undermining church attendances, subverting the morals of the young and encouraging sheer wicked time-wasting.

The work being done is either so microscopically detailed and technical or so general and sweeping in its assertions that it is hard to get a clear sight of the whole area from which to draw serviceable conclusions. Many scholars evince a curious diffidence about tackling the big issues which may be spiritually commendable but is practically crippling. Paul Soukup, after reviewing the literature on theology and communication, comments:

> The majority of authors cited call for some kind of systematic reflection on the relation between communication and theology

– either on the theoretical level or in terms of church practice. But then each disclaims the ability to engage this task. Whether this rhetorical humility is well-founded or whether it bespeaks an unwillingness to attempt the project leaves the same result; there are many beginnings but no comprehensive work.[48]

The literature on theology and communication may be shrouded in semantic fog, but what emerges through the gloom is a ghostly outline of the richness and variety of God's revelatory initiatives. The heading of the previous section – 'The Talkative God' – is much too restrictive. God is not just talkative; His gracious self-disclosure is bodied forth as well as bellowed forth. He engages more than the ears of people – as the Epistle of John puts it, 'that which we have heard, which we have seen with our eyes, which we have looked upon and touched with our hands, we declare unto you . . .'

Like lepidopterists leaping around with their butterfly-nets, we students of communication try to pin down this Scarlet Pimpernel of a God who is here, there and everywhere disclosing Himself – and always in three dimensions and teasing all the human senses. The Bible could have told us that, of course. He could be smelt in the smoke on Mount Horeb; heard in the still, small voice; tasted and found gracious by the Psalmist; touched by His garment's hem in Galilee; and above all, seen – in apparitions and visions and dreams and finally in human form.

Above all, seen. Aristotle said, 'of all the senses, trust only sight'. Revelation in the Bible certainly seems to elevate the image above the word – as Job said, 'I had heard of thee by the hearing of the ear; but now mine eye seeth thee . . .' And that apparently clinched the matter, though it would be fair to say that the word was the *standard* pattern of religious communication – the Gospel, says Ernst Fuchs, was a 'speech-event'.

Nevertheless, the image offers instantaneous disclosure whereas the story told takes time to unfold. It suffers less distortion than the word which is always a fragment of interrupted discourse and can mean many things; hence, the

scribes in the Bible did a roaring trade interpreting texts and
mediating the tradition. The combination of word and
image is most powerful of all as Jeremiah discovered when
confronted by the vision of the almond tree's rod – 'You have
seen well,' says God. 'I will hasten my word to perform it!'

It is a crashing truism to claim that the world is the theatre
of God's self-disclosure; that here the deeds of God are
reflected as in a mirror; that here the twin languages of
revelation are spoken and projected – things heard and
things seen. Since there is no more powerful vehicle in the
world for combining image and word than television, there
seems no obvious reason why the medium ought not to be
affirmed as a rich source of the stuff of natural theology.

The natural theologian plies an unfashionable trade these
days, looking for divine footprints in the sands of time, to the
hoots of detractors who claim with justice that the God of the
Gaps is a discredited deity. The mocking laughter has been a
little muted of late as scientists working on the far frontiers
of human knowledge have been describing their discoveries
in language that has more wild poetry than cool precision
about it. Because these grave savants propose for universal
building-blocks entities just about as substantial as moon-
beams, the whole spirit-matter business has got gloriously
muddled up again.

It could be charged that the reality perceived by courtesy of
the cathode ray tube is second-hand. But throughout history,
the majority of people have learned about God's work in the
world at second-hand. The Israelites assembled on the plain
to listen eagerly to the prophet's account of what he had seen
and heard on the mountain-top; they showed no disposition
to go up and see for themselves. Victorian Christians
crowded the chapels and public halls to hear returned
missionaries extol what God had done in distant lands
among an alien people. They didn't withhold their
hallelujahs until the era of the package tour enabled them to
test the truth.

There's just a touch of nostalgia or even intellectual
snobbery about our disposition to trust the classical journals
of exploration but to discount 'Whicker's World',

'Panorama' or 'Survival'. We get a more comprehensive view of the dimensions, density and variety of the world through the television screen than our forebears could possibly have had. Because of electronic technology the world implodes upon us. It enters us; we do not have to go out beyond the horizon to find it.

Certainly the view of the world as seen on television suffers from a statutory proportion of distortions; much of this book has been concerned with pointing out as much. But the pain we feel when watching a documentary about refugees in Somalia is real enough as is the sense of awe engendered by pictures beamed live to earth from the space shuttle. And not just serious stuff – belly laughter at knockabout comedy or heated involvement in televised sport – all such honest emotions constitute what Peter Berger might call signals of transcendence.

It assuredly looks a humanoid-dominated world that we glimpse through television. The values communicated are often highly ambiguous and we wriggle when we have the uncomfortable or even angry feeling we are being manipulated. But this is the way life is – highly ambiguous, most of the time opaque in meaning, abounding in paradox and irony, and a certain amount of it pretty shabby. The TV screen is not made of stained glass.

If our experience were transparent in meaning and could be dissolved without remainder into images and words which captured its essence exactly, we should have no need of any kind of theology, nor of faith either. From representations of life, symbols would then become substitutes for it – disbelief would be madness and reflection a waste of time.

There is, after all, a balancing and even challenging perspective built into the television experience. One role of religious broadcasting is to present the Gospel – which is a secular announcement that engages with other interpretations of history and life. As the electronic stream of consciousness flows by, that Gospel which confronts history from within – even from within the television screens – offers the viewer its stories of hope and justice, trust and freedom, invitation and decision.

So the ambiguities apparent throughout the television experience are not cause for unalloyed gloom; there is mystery swirling around the edges of the materialism. All the perennial questions about meaning and purpose and destiny still hover, waiting to be asked, as the mass media thrust the world at us through our eyes and ears for many hours a day.

Back to Square One

The crisis in Christian communication caused by the rise of the electronic media cannot possibly be more earth-shattering than Christianity's arrival on the scene in the first place. What can be learned about the Gospel as communication by going back to square one and studying Christian origins?

Historians have made much of the *praeparatio evangelica,* the combination of circumstances which meant that Christ arrived at a golden moment. Besides the essential preparation within the hearts of the people of God there was the *Pax Romana,* which included public order, a network of reasonable roads to permit easy travel and a community of language in varieties of Latin and Greek. The apostles were able to reach the maximum number of communities and address them with some hope of being understood. Among other things, the *Pax Romana* was a common communications environment, technologically achieved.

So are the electronic media. At a time of political and cultural pluralism, they will pass as surrogates for a *Pax Romana* – universal access, common language, widespread credibility. Even the key questions are similar – about the *praeparatio evangelica* within the people of God; the nature of the message when the medium is novel and how one affects the other; and the promise and challenge of a religious climate in which the old myths are dying, creating intellectual confusion and exposing raw superstition.

The precedent for using any cultural tools that come to hand and exploiting new technology is clearly set by the early Church. Amos Wilder quotes E.J. Goodspeed to the effect that the early Christians were among the first to use the book in the form of the codex, a primitive volume of manuscripts, in place of the scroll. Goodspeed writes:

> Christian books were copied and distributed on a scale no other ancient writings remotely approached... The early Christians were to an unusual extent a book-buying and book-reading people. They were also a translating and publishing people.[49]

Wilder also points out the intriguing fact that the ordinary papyrus scroll measured thirty feet, which was just about the right length for the longer Gospels, Matthew and Luke or the Acts of the Apostles. He contrasts the brevity of the New Testament books with the prolixity of the sacred writings of other religions but insists that this must have been determined by the needs of revelation rather than mechanical considerations about the length and portability of scrolls.

Nevertheless, this thought once put is illuminating. Every author must to some extent subordinate his message to the technical demands of the medium – manuscript length to book size, number of units to the extent of the print run. The invention of the paperback made books much more accessible to the general public because they were cheaper to buy and easier to carry. It is not an irreverent notion that the New Testament writers launched a first century version of the paperback at the cost of a certain creative discipline; it is a salute to a brilliant innovation in communication. And the moral surely is that the medium can be exploited for the message's sake, but always at the price of bending to its technical requirements.

Much less controversial and generally accepted is the recognition that the early Church pioneered new styles of literary form – the gospel, epistle and Johannine apocalypse. Christian rhetoric was a new utterance, both liberating language and renewing it. And it was a community product – the message was moulded by certain social patterns and reflected the emergence of a new society.

The Christian story told by some individual was thought about and prayed over by a fellowship, and a gospel was the result. The idea that inerrant words dropped from heaven, formed themselves into sentences and became the Gospel without being touched by human hands or cultural conditioning is now generally discredited – except in Salt Lake City. But it may be that the role of communications technology in shaping the structure of the Gospel needs much more careful investigation.

The general vigour and innovatory skill of the early Church in both using what media were available and inventing others must be positive endorsement of our attempts to do the same. As Amos Wilder puts it:

> Christian speech eventually laid hold of artistic media of communication current in paganism. But every step of the way, beginning with Jesus himself, represents an identification with and renewal of existing idioms. In one sense, as language, the Gospel met every man and each people where they were – was 'all things to all men' – in another sense it spoke a new word to all.

'The Gospel met every man and each people where they were' – and where they are now is at the centre of a nexus of electronic communications. And there are no grounds in Christian origins for disavowing television or radio as legitimate carriers of the Gospel. From the outset sacred languages were eschewed in favour of the idiom of the day. Jesus spoke Aramaic and Paul used koine Greek, the languages of the widest publics. It is true that the sheer novelty of the Gospel sometimes broke out of the conventions of language altogether and 'speaking with tongues' resulted. But there is no record of Jesus indulging in *glossolalia*.

The early Church knew nothing of any 'language of Zion' with a particular pietistic vocabulary and imagery. By analogy, the language of the electronic media cannot be castigated as too profane or worldly to bear the freight of the words of life. If the word-imagery of television is a true vernacular, then it is eligible. Spoken word, codex, printed page, televisual image – there is only one test; to paraphrase Abraham Lincoln, is this the language of the people by the people for the people?

The early Church was a community of story-tellers. They got that habit, of course, from the Old Testament, which had little to say about philosophical notions and instead told stories about miraculous beginnings, floods, burning bushes, sacred mountains, exoduses and exiles.[50] The first Christians endlessly told a story about victory over death. While the Christian intelligentsia attacked polytheism and made use of the ideas of contemporary philosophy such as the *logos* to build a cultural bridge to intellectual non-believers, simple disciples went on telling the same story to their children, to casual contacts and all they met in the street. Sailors carried the tale off to distant ports and slaves told their masters.

Professor Greenslade[51] says that much of the primitive Christian preaching was moralistic, trite and rather dull, though always based on the Bible. The missionary success of the apostles and their successors was founded on the perennial recitation of the story of God's dealings with man. The Gospel was brief, urgent in tone and free from the word-play and overblown rhetoric of pagan orators. And it could also be easily memorised.

There may be a clue here to a way round the problem of doing theology on television. If the medium resists those styles of theology based on propositions and abstract concepts, might there be a way forward through what is now called narrative theology – theology as story? For television is an electronic story-teller. It feeds on stories and casts chunks of material in narrative form in order to deal with them effectively.

It is not just drama and comedy, which are traditionally expressed in story form, that television treats as narrative. Most of the output is moulded in a style which demands action, development, conflict and resolution – document-aries, studio discussions, news-bulletins, even weather forecasts.

The shaping of programmes as narratives, with a beginning, middle and end, is made inevitable by the time-constraints and scheduling patterns by which television operates. There can be no loose ends, no jagged edges – one programme must be wrapped up to the viewer's satisfaction to make way for the next which will almost certainly be about an entirely different subject.

Significantly, every television programme is controlled by two scripts – a script for the words and a camera-script, for the cameras have their own tale to tell. Since pointless camera movement is thought technically crass, there is a theme to be traced in the tracking of the cameras which counterpoints that of the words and action of the programme.

In its simplest form, the television narrative is set out in testimony – 'One Pair of Eyes', 'Light of Experience', 'Yesterday's Witness', 'Our Reporter on the Spot', and so on. By some strange alchemy, the first-person narrative seems to overcome the distortions of the medium because the viewer perceives what Turgenev called 'the living truth of the human face'. In television on the grand scale, director and producer orchestrate the narrative through a complex interplay of film and video, studio and outside broadcast. But always the camera has an eye for spectacle, action, crisis, denouement.

Television is narrative and there is always a story-teller, even when no presenter or reporter is visible and in spite of the fact there may not be any commentary whatever. Someone is telling the story, has visualised the action, rendered it into shape and reflected on its outcome – if not a producer then a film editor or a cameraman; but there is always some controlling intelligence. That, plus a house-style, stern critics might call it a covert managerial ideology, which frames the output and puts a stamp on it as distinctive as a publisher's colophon.

It is the purpose of theology to enable the Gospel to be heard in any particular time, a formidable task which is often characterised by modest expressions such as tilling the ground, taking soundings and shifting the rubble to lay bare foundations. Television can be recruited to such a ground-clearing operation and used to tell stories which fulfil the function of the parables of Jesus – address people totally by 'keeping in solution' the language, belief and life of the

Kingdom – to use Dr Sally TeSelle's evocative phrase.

There is a wide range of television genres apt for this task, pre-eminently drama, which has a formidable pedigree as the primary vehicle for conveying the story of humanity's profoundest and silliest experiences. And it is a style endorsed in the Bible. Writes Amos Wilder:

> It is significant how large a place the dramatic mode has in the faith of the Bible and its forms of expression, even though we find no theatre-art as we know it in the Bible or amongst early believers. The important role of religious drama (in Christian witness) today has, nevertheless, specific justification in Biblical theology . . .[52]

But to introduce a grossly materialistic note into the discussion, drama is the most expensive form of television and the most demanding on a whole range of scarce human and technical resources. It is greedy of time and studio space. And since religious departments tend to be among the smallest and poorest sectors of the television operation, the opportunities for exploiting religious drama are strictly curtailed. BBC Television which has the largest religious staff of any television service known to me has only been able to mount three major drama productions in the past five years – a dramatised life of the blind Cornish poet, Jack Clemo, a reconstruction of a famous blasphemy trial at the Old Bailey and an hour-long drama about Martin Luther's conversion experience to celebrate the five hundredth anniversary of his birth.

So religious television must find other ways of telling its stories – through testimony, documentary and in the liturgical structure of worship. But there is still the whole corpus of general television drama on which to draw as the source material for reflection. The dominant themes of contemporary drama are rarely overtly religious, which is not surprising in an intensively secularised culture. Anyway, traditional Christian symbols and broadcasting are, alas, contradictions in terms. For broadcasting is about the stories and images which have near-universal acceptance, and Christian symbols have met that requirement only once in history – during the medieval period in Western Europe.

Nevertheless, as Dr F.W. Dillistone has pointed out, there are certain deep emotional needs which human beings seek to satisfy always and in every age:

> The security of relationship with one whose care and concern can be firmly relied upon;
> the freedom for growth and expansion towards definite fulfilment;
> the sense of an ordered framework within which life in community can be established in justice and peace;
> the discovery of guidance towards the unfolding of the ultimate meaning of existence.[53]

At different times and in various places, one or other of these needs may assume a disproportionate significance, but overall, the human organism yearns to hear stories or to relate to symbols which point to the realisation of these goals. For Dr Dillistone, the symbol which gathers up all these concerns is that of the living Christ made visible and audible on television through stories about His followers caring, venturing, suffering and witnessing.

Since Dr Dillistone wrote those words religious broadcasting has become less consciously Christocentric. This is not because the miasma of religious scepticism has seeped under the doors of Broadcasting House or the Television Centre, but because programmes must try to answer the needs of a multi-religious society. Religious broadcasters who are Christians must invoke Bonhoeffer's anonymous Christ known by many names and none, and settle for the transcendent as the code-word which triggers response in followers of the great religious traditions. But Dr Dillistone's account of the four basic emotional needs of the human being still offer an ambitious agenda for television producers seeking to illuminate the human condition.

Theology as story has two obvious themes. There is the miraculous turn of grace expressed through the great polarities of life – decay and renewal, death and resurrection, being lost and then found. The Gospel, claimed J.R.R. Tolkien, is the fairy tale which encompasses all fairy tales. It is the story everyone hopes to find true.[54] There is also the theme of travel. Every story is about a journey, in space, time or condition. The classical pattern was succinctly set out in Dr W.E. Sangster's homiletical structure for dealing with the parable of the prodigal son – Sick of Home; Homesick; Home. The journey is inspired by a crisis, is sustained by faith, hope and love and culminates in a great fireworks display of welcome at the destination.

Possibly the key difference between narrative-theology and its more formal stable-mates is that it deals with the theme of coming to belief rather than the beliefs themselves. Coming to belief is a story; examining beliefs is an intellectual exercise. There is perpetual fascination in observing the titanic struggle of a human being thrusting forward through fog to the light on the rim of the horizon. Most people can identify with the theme, even those who gave up at some point and settled for life in semi-gloom. There is rich source-material for religious television in this theological idiom.

An Afterword on Body-snatching
There is one feature of the earliest Christian speech, including that of Jesus himself, which is both a warning and a reproach to those of us who seek to use the mass media for religious communication – it was extempore, unstudied, aimed for the immediate moment without concern for its longer-term effect. Jesus did not speak for posterity's sake in words carefully sculpted for recording and storage. For Him and for the apostles, the standard locus for communicating the Gospel was face-to-face encounter.

> The Gospel meant freedom of speech in this deeper sense. One did not hoard its formulas, since when occasion arose, the Spirit would teach one what to say and how to witness and what defence to make. The earliest Christians lived on the free bounty of God in this sense also. The speech of the Gospel was thus fresh and its forms novel and fluid; it came and went, as Ernst Fuchs says, with the freedom of sunshine, wind and rain.[55]

The word of the Gospel was always incarnate, embodied

in the person of the messenger so that hearers could judge the worth of both together – the speaker and what was said. It was the Gnostics who were the body-snatchers of the first centuries of the Christian era. They wished to distil the human spirit out from its fleshly accretions so that it might grasp perfect truth. The early Christians would have none of it – truth had to be expressed through fully human encounter.

As I have shown, Gnosticism has taken on a new lease of life with the advent of broadcasting. We broadcasters are the body-snatchers of our time. We take flesh and blood human beings, place them in front of a camera or microphone and turn them into disembodied voices or depersonalised images. This is putting the Johannine assertion that the Word became flesh into reverse. We take flesh and blood human beings and spiritualise them into words.

We even strive for a gnostic perfection in producing that disembodied voice. Though the wiliest broadcasters permit a statutory percentage of imperfection in their recordings, the rest edit out every error, fluff and hesitation to make a tape as pure as possible. No truly human voice ever spoke in such measured cadences with exact intonations, immaculate to the last syllable. This is like the unearthly purity which was the Gnostics' goal.

There is an almost irresistible but illicit form of power in the disembodied voice across the ether. In 1958, when I was a missionary in what was then Northern Rhodesia, the Government decreed that part of the Gwembe Valley should be flooded to enlarge Lake Kariba. The story goes that the Paramount Chief of the tribe in the Valley addressed his people and told them of the splendid new houses and gardens awaiting them on the high ground. The people murmured angrily, turned away and would not move. A few days later, the Paramount Chief's appeal was broadcast from Radio Lusaka. The people heard it and moved away without further protest.

Why? The Valley people did not think of the radio as some form of magic; they'd been accustomed to it for years. But there was a compelling authority in the disembodied voice.

Edmund Carpenter, the social anthropologist, noted the same phenomenon in a different cultural setting. 'I knew a Californian who read his poetry aloud at parties until his friends learned to silence him. But when he played recordings of these same poems, everyone listened.'

The McLuhan model of communications techniques as extensions of the human senses suggest the outline of a great, ghostly, gnostic being with print and camera for eyes, telephone and radio for ears and a central nervous system made up of miscellaneous electronic devices. Thus we can magnify the impact of the Gospel to an extent undreamed of by Jesus and the earliest Christians. There is, however, one crucial difference. It is speech without speaker, image without presence, contact without personal engagement.

By courtesy of mass media, we Christian communicators can tell the whole world about the love of God without its costing us anything more than the expenditure of a little technique and a lot of breath. It is love at a distance; at the other end of the microphone, camera or printing press. No one can tap us on the shoulder and say, 'Prove it!' We are beyond reach. The act of broadcasting, however sincerely executed, tears apart the unity of word and action personified in and by Jesus.

Is it an utterly outrageous thought that something fundamental in Christianity changed, and not for the better, when one person need no longer look another person in the eye and say, 'Let me tell you about Jesus,' and instead could suggest, 'Read this!' or 'Watch this!' or 'Listen to this!'?

There is a paradox here that cannot be fully resolved. The religious broadcaster must conjure with the truth that *every* method of conveying the Gospel other than face-to-face encounter is defective. It is our occupational thorn in the flesh.

And if the Incarnation is one doctrine against which religious broadcasters stub their toes, the doctrine of the Cross is the other. The Cross symbolises the power of God made perfect in earthly impotence. The Gospel makes its appeal from earthly weakness to earthly strength; it is preached from the Cross to the secular powers.

The relationship of the media to their viewers and listeners is the precise opposite. They are immense power-sources, addressing their publics from positions of dominating influence. Whatever is communicated by television and radio is being transmitted from strength to weakness, power to impotence, media-might to frail human listener or viewer. Granted, the hearer has the ultimate sanction in the flick of a switch. But it is one thing to have the ability; quite another to show the will.

The theologians talk about the *impassibility* of God by which they mean he is incapable of suffering, injury or emotion. The electronic media have their own pseudo god-like form of impassibility. We talk about radio and television *networks,* but they are more like one-way conduits through which a single source addresses many outlets. And the disembodied voice is impervious to the response of the outlets which are known with numbing accuracy as 'receivers'. Writes Gunther Anders, 'When the world speaks to us, without our being able to speak to it, we are deprived of speech and hence, condemned to be unfree.'

All the mass media are secular institutions of great potency, operating under only the very sketchiest of public control. They do not pretend to be democratic; ordinary people have virtually no sustained access to them except in token ways; and they dominate by the sheer pervasiveness of their influence over our lives. They are concentrations of those social, economic and cultural forces against which Jesus expressed the harshest of anathemas.

The Gospel of the Cross is the supreme example of non-dominating communication; indeed, it is communication by the dominated. The religious broadcaster is, therefore, confronted by an absurdity – trying to proclaim from a position of immense secular power the futility of secular power compared to the divine strength exhibited in utter weakness on the Cross. We are like a millionaire preaching the virtues of poverty from the back seat of a gold-plated Rolls.

A certain aura of romance, even glamour, attaches to those who work in the mass media, especially television with its immediacy, drama and vivid impact. If they happen to be religious broadcasters there is also spiritual harrowing; the numbing sense that much of what they do seems so alien to the spirit of Jesus, the shocking particularity of whose love mocks *mass* media or *mass* anything else. These Christians may attract envy; they need spiritual support.

NOTES

Introduction
1 Cole, *Television Today*, p.v. Oxford, 1981.
2 Toffler, *The Third Wave*, p.217. Pan, 1981.

Chapter One
3 My attention was drawn to this image by Gregory Battcock in *The New Television*, p.17 et seq. Mass. Inst. Tech. Press, n.d.
4 I owe this notion and analysis to: Fiske and Hartley, *Reading Television*, p.85 et seq. Methuen, 1978.
5 Quoted by Muggeridge, *Christ and the Media*, p.46. Hodder, 1977.
6 Novak in *Television as a Social Force*, p.9 et seq. Praeger, New York, 1975.
7 Ibid., p.12.

Chapter Two
8 *See* Vilem Flusser in *The New Television*, p.236 et seq. Mass. Inst. Tech. Press, n.d.
9 Carpenter, *Oh What a Blow that Phantom Gave Me!* p.145. Paladin, 1973.

Chapter Three
10 Papanek, *Design for the Real World*, p.72 et seq. Granada, 1974.
11 Rowlands in *The Third Age of Broadcasting*, p.88. Faber, 1982.

Chapter Four
12 *See* Miller's analysis in *McLuhan*. Fontana, 1970.
13 Boorstin in *Television Today*, p.256 et seq. Oxford, 1981.

Chapter Five
14 Unfortunately K. Wolfe's exhaustive *The Churches and the BBC 1922-1956* (SCM, 1984) had not been published when I wrote this chapter.
15 McKay, *Take Care of the Sense*, p.61 SCM, 1964.
16 Ibid., p.62.

Chapter Six
17 *Theology*, July 1983, p.259 et seq.

Chapter Seven
18 Quoted by Basil Mitchell in *Broadcasting, Society and the Church*. CIO, 1973.

Chapter Eight
19 Quoted by Colin McArthur in *Television and History*. BFI, 1978.
20 Phelan, *Mediaworld*, p.64. Seabury, N.Y., 1977.
21 McArthur, ibid.
22 Day, *Day by Day*, p.22. Kimber, 1975.
23 Muggeridge, *Christ and the Media*, p.32. Hodder, 1977.
24 I owe much of the analysis in this section to Phelan, *Mediaworld*, p.13 et seq.

Chapter Nine
25 Quoted by Dillistone, *Traditional Symbols and the Contemporary World*, p.2. Epworth, 1973.
26 *See* Raymond Williams, *Television: Technology and Cultural Form*, ch.5. Fontana, 1974.
27 Carpenter, *Oh What a Blow*, p.155. Paladin, 1973.
28 Dulles. *The Church is Communications*, p.16. Multimedia International, 1971.
29 Nineham, *The Use and Abuse of the Bible*, p.12f. Macmillan, 1976.
30 I have leaned very heavily in this section on the analysis in G. Goethals, *The TV Ritual*, p.84 et seq. Beacon Press, Boston, 1981.
31 Quoted by Goethals, ibid., p.143.
32 *See* Capo in *Media Development*, vol.xxx, p.10 et seq.
33 Quoted by Fernando Reyes Matta, *Media Development* vol. XXX, p.17.
34 Matta, ibid.

Chapter Ten
35 Granfield, *Ecclesial Cybernetics*. Macmillan, N.Y., 1973.
36 Quoted by Dulles, *Models of the Church*. Gill and Macmillan, 1976.
37 Ibid.
38 Quoted by Hadden and Swann, *Prime-Time Preachers*, p. 7-8. Addison-Wesley, Mass., 1981.
39 Horsfield, summarised in *Research Trends in Religious Communications*. CSCC, n.d.
40 Berger, *The Heretical Imperative*, p.52. Doubleday, 1979.
41 *See* Harned, *The Ambiguity of Religion*, p.123. Westminster, 1968.

Chapter Eleven
42 Dulles, *The Church is Communications*, p.8. Multimedia, 1971.
43 Heinrichs in *Media Development*, vol. XXVIII, p.6.
44 Webber, *God Still Speaks*, p.71. Nelson, 1981.
45 Quoted by Webber. Ibid.
46 Hamelink, *Perspectives for Public Communication*, p.49. Ten Have, 1975.
47 I owe this analysis to Paul Soukup, *Theology and Communication*, CSCC, 1982.
48 Ibid.
49 Wilder, *Early Christian Rhetoric*, p.16n. SCM, 1964.
50 Martin Marty in *Opening Eyes and Ears*, p.113. WCC, 1983.
51 Greenslade in unpublished monograph *Early Christian Preaching*.
52 Wilder, *Early Christian Rhetoric*, p.59 et seq. SCM. 1964.
53 Dillistone in an article whose source I cannot now trace.
54 Quoted by Navone, *Towards a Theology of Story*, p.24. St Paul's, 1977.
55 Wilder, *Early Christian Rhetoric*, p.21. SCM, 1964.

INDEX